For Christ in
Cambridge

For Christ in Cambridge

Charles Simeon

George F. MacLean

CF4·K

10 9 8 7 6 5 4 3 2 1

Copyright © 2022 George F. MacLean
Paperback ISBN: 978-1-5271-0841-7
Ebook ISBN: 978-1-5271-0911-7

Published by Christian Focus Publications,
Geanies House, Fearn, Tain, Ross-shire,
IV20 1TW, Scotland, U.K.
www.christianfocus.com;
email: info@christianfocus.com

Cover design by Daniel van Straaten
Cover illustration by Daniel van Straaten
Printed and bound by Nørhaven, Denmark

Scripture quotations are from the King James Version.

Contents

To our dear grandchildren
Hannah and Jonathan

Foreword

Do you have a Christian club in your school? Can you meet with others who are interested in the Bible and Jesus and find out more about the Christian faith? That is a really helpful thing for young Christians.

It is interesting that when we look up the Wikipedia entry on the Internet for Eton College, the most famous school in the U.K., we learn that there is a Christian club in the school called Simeon. Why is it called Simeon? Well, this book will help you work that out, because the name comes from Charles Simeon, who died in 1836. Not many of us will have something named after us, so he must have been special in some way. But often the name of a person can live on – in the name of a street, for example, – but the person can be forgotten. I hope you agree when you have read this book that Charles Simeon should not be forgotten. Enjoy reading about him.

Early Years

It was a cold, raw, still January day outside Eton College. The clatter of hooves could be heard from a distance as a plush carriage drawn by four bay horses approached the entrance to the impressive buildings. With a loud 'Whoa!' the driver pulled on the reins. With much snorting and stamping, the steaming horses came to a stop. A carriage door swung open. Out jumped an agile seven-year-old boy. He gazed at the red-brown and honey-coloured stone, the high castellated[1] tops to the walls and the spire-topped towers. What is this place going to be like? he thought to himself. A shiver may not have been totally due to the penetrating damp.

'Come on, Charles. Look smart or your masters will get a bad impression of you.'

'Yes, Father.'

They proceeded to the entrance followed by a servant lugging a compact, but heavy, leather trunk with C. Simeon stencilled on the side. Charles's father pulled his heavy blue woollen coat around him. The

---

1. Like a castle.

wide heavy sleeves ornamented with silver buttons and the cream silk breeches showed his status as a man of property and influence.

A tall man with a sharp nose, dressed in black except for a grey waistcoat, hastened out. 'Ah, Richard Simeon, Esquire, I believe. We were expecting you. You are very welcome. I am Mr John Foster, Headmaster of Eton College. Did you have a good journey?'

'Tolerable. The carriage is well sprung.'

'And what is your name, boy?'

Charles looked up into the piecing blue eyes. 'Charles Simeon, sir.'

'I trust you will work hard and be a credit to Eton College and your family. Come this way. I will introduce Charles to his house master and you and I, Mr Simeon, shall partake of some tea – quite the fashion nowadays, I believe.'

The little group of three proceeded off into the interior of the building, Charles two or three steps behind the adults, gazing around him.

* * *

Charles Simeon was the fourth and youngest son of successful businessman and landowner Richard Simeon. He was born in Reading, approximately forty miles west of London, on 24th September, 1759. Though baptised as was expected in those days, he was not brought up in a home where religion was important or strictly observed, despite both parents having ancestors who held important positions in the

Church of England. Sadly, his mother died when he was a young child and he scarcely had any recollection of her. Although he had a privileged and well-to-do background, life at Eton would not be a bed of roses.

* * *

Charles sat on the hard wooden bench conscious of the stares of boys curious about the newcomer or just waiting to pounce on some weakness, ready to attach to him a cutting nickname.

'What's for supper?' he asked the boy next to him.

'Just the usual mutton scraps left over from dinner,' answered the boy without glancing at him.

'That doesn't seem very appealing.'

'It's what we get every day. Mashed potato and mutton at two o'clock with the scraps at six.'

'What if you don't like mutton?'

'Then you go hungry.'

'When is breakfast?'

'Ten o'clock. You get milk and a buttered roll. Same at ten at night.'

'No breakfast till ten o'clock! I'll be famished by then!'

'You'll get used to it.'

* * *

The boy's prophecy proved correct. Charles endured not only the unvaried diet (Eton College had land which supported a large flock of sheep) but also the unimaginative teaching, drudgery and harsh discipline.

Latin and, to a much lesser extent, Greek were the subjects taught. Learning by heart was the teaching method. Pupils were also introduced to the wisdom and mythologies[2] of the Roman and Greek past, which may have been more interesting for them. They slept in a long dormitory, a room containing fifty beds. Each junior pupil was assigned to a senior boy who was entitled to ask him to do humdrum tasks such as cleaning shoes or making beds. This drudgery was called 'fagging'. Failure to do these tasks properly could result in painful discipline. The masters, too, frequently beat boys for a range of offences. One thing which Eton College emphasised was fitness and various rough team games were part of school life.

Charles developed over the years in Eton into an athletic youth.

* * *

'Hi there, fellows. That was a jolly good game of cricket. Beats translating the Aeneid[3].'

'Yes. This college needs livening up. Show one of your party tricks, Charles.'

'I'd love to. Say, Josiah, you arrange the chairs.'

Josiah knew what was expected of him. He arranged six chairs in a row. 'Rather you than me,' he said. 'I'd break my neck.'

---

2. Stories of gods and heroes which are usually far-fetched.
3. The Aeneid is a Latin Epic poem written by Virgil between 29 and 19 B.C.

Charles took a deep breath, sprang forward and with one bound cleared the six chairs.

There were shouts of, 'Bravo, Charles!' and much clapping from the half dozen classmates.

'What about the candle trick?' asked Trevor.

'See if you can get a candle, then.'

While Trevor sauntered off to find a candle, Charles took off his shoes and silk stockings. He had started to dress in a vain, show-off manner. (Men in those times, especially the well-off, might dress in splendidly embroidered silk waistcoats, wear shirts with frilly cuffs and sport cut-away coats with craftsmen-designed silver buttons.)

Trevor entered slowly with the lit candle in a sconce[4] so that the flame would not flicker and go out.

'Okay, Trevor, put it on the floor.'

When Trevor put the sconce on the floor, without hesitation, Charles snuffed out the candle with his toes, again to clapping and cheers.

Never the most handsome of boys, his ability in horse-riding and games and his party tricks made him well-accepted at Eton, despite being mocked for his flashy dress sense.

So what about the Christian faith, because Eton was originally closely linked to the parish church? Was Charles a follower of Jesus at this time? Prayers were said three times a day in Latin and chapel services were held, but all was routine and lifeless. The only

---

4. A candlestick holder with a handle.

spark of religious interest shown by Charles was when there was a national fast day during the American War of Independence. He took that seriously and only ate one hard-boiled egg all day. However, his fellow Etonians thought this was more in tune with his show-off character than genuine religious conviction – and they were proved correct as this religious turn was very temporary. Sometimes he did show flashes of conscience and kept a money box for the poor. But that was just a sop to his conscience, not love learnt from the heart of God.

Cambridge and Conversion

The nineteen-year-old Charles gazed through the January mist rising from the River Cam at the magnificent King's College Chapel with its spires, huge stained glass windows and high stone vaulted ceilings, an outstanding achievement of late medieval architecture and craftsmanship. With two other 'freshmen' – meaning new students – called Joseph Goodall and William Moore he had started out on academic life. All three were from Eton, as King's College only took students from that source. There were only about fifteen other students in King's College who were yet to complete their studies and graduate.

Joseph Goodall broke the awed silence. 'Well, we'll see plenty of this place. Prayers twice a day.'

'Much good will it do my soul – if I have one,' muttered William Moore sourly.

'Well, we had them three times a day in Eton,' responded Charles.

'And much good they did you, Charles – unless horsemanship and vanity qualify you for heaven!'

'William, your tongue will get you into trouble. Never mind, I'm looking forward to a proper breakfast, not the miserable fare in Eton.'

'Yes, Charles,' answered Joseph, 'I hear some people have toast and crumpets and eggs and butter followed by ham or chicken with tea or coffee and honey or marmalade to finish.'

'Trust you two to be thinking of your stomachs. Are you fixed up with servants?' asked William.

'Yes, William. They seem reliable. I have a male servant, a coal-carrier and a bed-maker. Oh, and you'll love this – I have arranged for a barber to see to my wigs.'

'Trust you, Charles,' chimed the other two.

* * *

A town of seven to eight thousand people, Cambridge was surrounded by fields and marshy land which abounded in game birds. Roads were rutted and potholed. There was no street lighting, or pavements or drains. Streets were cobbled and extremely narrow. The River Cam, or Granta as it originally was called, was a busy commercial waterway. Horses waded shoulder high up the river from King's Lynn on the coast pulling barges laden with goods such as butter and coal.

* * *

Charles splashed his way down Bennet Street. It was a dreary, wet day. Suddenly his eye was attracted to a small queue outside a shop.

'What is the queue for?' he asked.

'Oh,' replied the man at the back of the queue, 'this shop has the only umbrellas in town and hires them out. I hate getting my wig wet. It takes such an age for the servant to get it dried out.'

'An umbrella? What's that?'

'Oh, it is like a cane or stick with material almost like webbing at the top which folds down when there is no rain. They are common in France, but people don't like French things – they support the rebel Americans.'

'That wouldn't bother me. I am going to buy one.'

And buy one he did, which added to his fashionable image. (This umbrella is still to be seen in a glass case in his former church in Cambridge called Holy Trinity.)

* * *

Cambridge University had some famous scholars at the time, but the general standard of teaching was sub-standard and an easy-going, lackadaisical[1] attitude prevailed. This probably affected Charles because he loved horse-riding, dancing, cricket and swimming among other activities. On one occasion, he and a companion rode part of the way to a Monday dance on the Lord's Day. In those days the Sabbath was generally well kept. They stopped off at a friend's house for refreshments with the result that Charles became intoxicated. The horse, wiser than Charles and his companion, turned in at an inn, where the innkeeper made them stay for the night until he had recovered.

1. Half-hearted.

On the way home, after the dance, the landlady of an inn said in innocence to Charles, 'Have you heard that a gentleman from Reading has been killed by a fall from his horse while drunk?' Reading was Charles's home town. The thought disturbed Charles. It could easily have been him.

* * *

Despite this outward careless abandonment to pleasure, there was an underlying unease in Charles. On the third day in his room, he was well-pleased. His room was in order. He had bought in a good stock of the best wine. Soon his coachman and horses would be settled in.

Knock, knock. Who was that at his door?

'Come in.'

It was the porter. 'This is a letter from the Provost[2] for you, Master Charles. I have given a letter each to Masters Joseph and William, too.'

'Thank you, porter. Here is a sixpence.'

'That's kind of you, master.'

I wonder what's in this letter? thought Charles. He opened the letter and read it slowly. *You are required to attend Holy Communion in King's College Chapel in three weeks' time.*

Charles had never partaken of the bread and wine representing the body and blood of the Lord Jesus. Careless though he had been, he recognised that this was a deeply spiritual act. He had scarcely ever given serious thought to matters of religion. But now there

---

2. Head of the college.

was no escape from attendance at Communion. Only Church of England members could take degrees in Cambridge. Most of those who taught were clergymen. All Cambridge students were required to receive Communion at least three times each year during their time at university.

The thought so gnawed at him that he turned to the only book he knew for help. It was called *The Whole Duty of Man,* but it was of no help. He began to feel dreadfully unworthy. He said that he frequently looked upon the dogs with envy. Presumably, this was because they could not sin and become guilty like he was. Later, he said of himself at that time, 'Satan himself was as fit to attend as I.' However, he so fasted and prayed and read, that he almost made himself ill. But attend he did. However, he knew that he had to attend again on Easter Sunday and the unease settled in again.

Then he discovered a book called *Instruction for the Lord's Supper* by Bishop Thomas Wilson. For two months he continued reading the book, which he found more helpful. How, though, could the sacrifice of Christ, depicted in the bread and wine, be effective in removing his guilt and unworthiness? How could he obtain peace with an offended God? How could he receive the tokens of God's love to him when his heart was not right with God? Eventually, Easter approached and he, in his state of spiritual turmoil, kept reading Bishop Wilson's book. Suddenly, a statement in the book jumped out of the page at him, as it were: *the Jews knew what they did when they transferred their sin to the head of their offering.* This referred to the rules laid down in the book of Leviticus in the Old Testament for animal sacrifices. The person making the offering held his hand on the head of the animal. This action taught that the animal represented the person and paid the penalty of death on behalf of that person. *What*, he thought, *I can transfer my guilt to Another! I will not bear them in my soul a moment longer.* Later he wrote: 'Accordingly, I sought to lay my sins upon the sacred head of Jesus; and on the Wednesday began to have hope of mercy; on the Thursday that hope increased; on the Friday and the Saturday it became more strong; and on the Sunday morning, Easter Day, 4th April, I awoke early with those words upon my heart and lips, "Jesus Christ is risen today! Hallelujah! Hallelujah!" From that hour, peace flowed in rich abundance into my soul and at the Lord's Table, in our Chapel, I had the sweetest access to God through my blessed Saviour.'

His guilt removed, his heart flooded with gospel peace, Charles nevertheless faced difficulties. He did not know one Christian in King's College with whom he could discuss his new-found faith. But, as his conversion had obviously been the work of the Spirit of God, so was his development as a believer. He rose each morning at 4 a.m. to study the Scriptures, to worship, confess his sin and pray. He also found the set prayers of the Anglican Prayer Book a blessing to his soul and always remained loyal to the Church of England. These times of personal devotion built him up in the faith, but he was not content with a private faith. Every Sunday evening he started to hold worship for his servants, hoping to do them spiritual good.

* * *

Sometimes, home can be the most difficult place to confess faith in Christ and be a true witness. Charles found that out when he made his way home to Reading for the long summer vacation.

The servants had with rapid efficiency cleared the long, highly polished mahogany table in the dining room. Richard, his eldest brother, sat looking rather sickly and staring into his wine. His other brother, Edward, had slipped out.

'Charles, what is this I hear about you conducting worship with the servants?' demanded his father.

Charles looked him in the eye. 'The reports you heard are quite correct. We are all God's creatures, Father, and worship is his due from everyone. Richard comes to the worship times and has no objection. We would be very pleased if you would grace us with your presence.'

'Harrumph! I fear that you are infected with the enthusiasm and fervour of the Methodists. Religion must be orderly and respectable. Now I hear that you are friendly with the Vicar of St Files in the town. He is one of those who stir people up with talk of sin and conversion and new birth and gets people to be forever reading their Bibles. Have nothing to do with him.'

'Father, I respect your wishes, but the servants have souls and spiritual needs. They are happy that I care for their souls. I will not preach for Mr Cadogan, the Vicar, but I will remain his friend.'

'Oh, all right then. Tell the servants to bring me more wine.'

* * *

Sadly, Charles's brother, Richard, took unwell and died young, but not before he professed faith in Christ. Charles's father never fell out with him but remained prejudiced towards what he considered an unbalanced and misguided religious outlook. Life continued at King's College back in Cambridge.

Perhaps, because he was isolated and lacked true Christian friends to give him an example, Charles only gradually realised his need to turn away from the sins and doubtful worldly pleasures which still characterised his new life as a Christian. Slowly he learned from his mistakes. Whenever his conscience was enlightened, he was very careful to realise his need for contrition and repentance. However, the vanity and quick temper, which were features of his life before conversion, were problems he wrestled with most of his days. Practices such as economising in order to devote some of his income to the Lord were quickly established from the beginning. The result was that he finished his three years of scholarship without owing as much as a shilling (five pence) yet supported the Lord's work. Self-discipline and perseverance were to stand him in good stead in the future.

Becoming a Preacher

At Cambridge at that time, academic gowns were important. The top group of students were from very privileged backgrounds. They wore gowns of purple, green, black or even rose with gold trimmings. They usually cared nothing for study and had a bad reputation for wild living. Most students had plain gowns. Students were called gownsmen. For Charles, however, this changed after three years when he became a Fellow. This was a title given to those who had completed their studies and it entitled the person to wear a more distinguished gown and to become a tutor or teacher. Strangely, students at King's College did not have to sit university examinations to become Fellows!

It also enabled him to move his rooms from the Old Court to much more spacious and comfortable accommodation in Gibb's Building (which was modern at the time as it had been added to King's College in 1724).

A year later, still at King's College, Charles became a deacon. This was his first official position in the Church of England. The ceremony in which a person becomes a deacon is called ordination. The nearest cathedral to Cambridge is in Ely, which is around fifteen miles away. Bishop James Yorke ordained him.

At that time, a newly ordained deacon had to find a posting. Bigger churches paid their ministers (known as vicars or rectors) what was called a living. Charles did not know how he could become an assistant to one of these. These assistants were called curates. He thought of putting an advert in the newspapers offering to serve a like-minded minister as a curate without payment. But God stepped in.

One Sunday, Charles was worshipping in a Cambridge church called St Edward's. As in other churches, he had no friends, but he enjoyed the preaching of Mr Christopher Atkinson, the vicar.

After the blessing had been pronounced at the end of the service, the vicar proceeded slowly down the aisle of the church. To Charles's surprise, he stopped at his pew.[1] 'I believe you are a gownsman at King's, young man. What is your name?'

Startled, Charles replied, 'Charles Simeon, sir. I enjoyed your sermon. It was very suited to me. I always feel myself so sinful and needy and you pointed me again to Jesus, the Lamb of God.'

'Oh,' said Mr Atkinson thoughtfully. He paused. 'Well, I am glad to hear that. I have a confession to make. I should have made your acquaintance earlier

---

1. A long wooden, bench-like seat in a church.

but somehow took it into my head that you were … shall we say, rather self-righteous? I am glad that I have been proved by your words to have totally misjudged you. Please accept my apology.'

'Oh, don't apologise, sir. I am sure there is more than a bit of the Pharisee about me yet.'

'Well, I was the one guilty of judging, Charles. Do you know many people in our congregation?'

'I haven't any real Christian friends, sir.'

'Well, I think I can help there. Come and I will introduce you to a fine young man.' He led Charles over to where a friendly-looking man stood talking to others.

'John, may I introduce you to Charles Simeon, a King's gownsman and a believer.'

'I am delighted to meet you, Charles. King's, eh? Not many Christians there, I hear.'

'None that I have discovered. What's your college?'

'Sidney Sussex. I graduated last year and am preparing for an M.A. My father is Rector of Yelling, which is about twelve miles away. Would you like to come over and join us when I am at home?'

'I would love that.'

'I think you two will get on very well,' commented Mr Atkinson. 'Now, Charles, I have been looking for a stand-in curate for the summer. Would you like to consider this? I am afraid it would have to be an honorary[2] post as we are not a wealthy congregation.'

---

2. Unpaid.

'Sir, I am quite astonished at your kind offer. It is the Lord's provision. I would love to gain experience of ministering in the church, as so far I have only been able to lead household worship.'

'Consider it done then, Charles.'

John Venn's invitation was accepted, too. Charles and John spent time there with John's father, Henry Venn, who had exercised a powerful ministry in Huddersfield, Yorkshire and then moved to Yelling. After a pleasant afternoon in the company of John's father and his three sisters, they rode back to Cambridge.

* * *

Now that Charles Simeon was gone, the sisters burst out in uncontrollable laughter among themselves.

'Oh, my dear girls, what is the matter?' questioned a perplexed Henry Venn.

'It's Mister Simeon. He is so odd and awkward. His chin protrudes. He grimaces[3] strangely. When he talks, he doesn't just talk – he lectures. I could hardly look at him.'

The daughters tittered and giggled again. Henry Venn frowned a little and then said to them, 'Come with me, my dears, out into the garden.'

They obediently followed their ageing father. He led them up to a peach tree in the well-tended garden. It was early summer and everything was growing lush.'

'Now pick me one of those peaches.'

---

3. Twists his face.

'But father, they are still green. It's far too early for peaches to ripen. Even the strawberries haven't properly ripened.'

Henry Venn's face crinkled as he smiled gently. 'Don't you see the point? The fruit is green now and we must wait, but a little more sun and a few more showers, and the peach will ripen and be sweet. So it is with Mr Simeon.'

The daughters looked embarrassed. 'Father, we have been silly. We needed that lesson,' said his daughter, Eling, quietly.

Charles came to love riding out to Yelling and learning from the experience and godly wisdom and kindness of Henry Venn, who was to be a father-figure to him. John Venn was himself to became the Rector of Clapham Church in London and a leading figure in the evangelical[4] Clapham Sect which was prominent in the anti-slavery movement. Through the connection with the Venns, Charles was to be introduced to leading evangelical figures and lose his isolation.

* * *

Charles' buckled shoes clattered on the cobbles of the narrow Cambridge street, where he was visiting door-to-door. The area was where nearly all the local butchers had their quarters. It was poor and rather squalid. Suddenly, a hubbub of roaring

---

4. Christians who believed strongly in the Bible and preaching the need for conversion and being changed by God the Holy Spirit.

and yelling burst out from one house. Screams and swearing rent the air. Startled, but unconcerned, Charles knocked with his cane on the door and strode into the house.

'What is all this racket?' he demanded sternly. 'Who is daring to offend Almighty God with these horrendous swears?'

The culprits were silenced. Who was this intruder on their domestic ding-dong? 'Who are you, mister?' asked the man. 'I don't see that you should be butting in on a little quarrel we were having, me and my missus.'

'I am the parish curate for the summer. I have every right to visit every household in the parish and from what I have heard you have every need of my visit. Do you not fear God when you use such dreadful language and treat your wife like this? Your tongues were made to praise God, not to shout and screech at one another. Now, on your knees, and I will pray to God for your forgiveness.'

Husband and wife glanced at each other. Neither dared challenge this zealous curate. Down they knelt.

'Almighty God, show us our sinfulness and the blackness of our hearts. How can we stand before a God who is light and holiness? But we give thanks for Jesus who shed his blood on the cross. His blood alone can wash away our sins. Cleanse the hearts of these two sinners here, cleanse their tongues and help them to seek mercy. Bless this household with peace. Amen.'

'Bless you, sir. My hubby and myself lost our senses just now and we are sorry. Isn't that right, Harry?'

'Aye, that's right, Eliza. It's right good of you to pray for us, curate. I reckon we need your prayers.'

'Well, I came in God's time. Now remember – my prayers will do you no good unless you pray for yourselves. Pray for mercy. Pray for new hearts.'

As Charles stepped out of the gloom of the house, he saw that a small crowd of curious onlookers had gathered. Never the one to pass by an opportunity, he said to them, 'You have seen that the gospel brings peace. Jesus brings peace and forgiveness. He brings God into our lives. Come and hear me preach the gospel on Sunday. It is the power of God to salvation. Now go to your homes.'

Wondering about this new curate, who was prepared to brave a ferocious domestic row, the onlookers slowly dispersed.

* * *

After seventeen weeks as an unpaid curate, Charles's zealous preaching had made a real mark. The small church was filled to overflowing. One person commented that it was 'crowded like a theatre on the first night of a new play'. The pews overflowed, the aisles were packed and the Parish Clerk's seat was taken. When the vicar returned to St Edward's, the Parish Clerk said to him, with a sigh of relief, 'Oh, sir, I am so glad you are come; now we shall have some room!' – perhaps not realising that he was not paying the vicar much of a compliment.

* * *

Being introduced to John Venn and gaining experience in pastoral work and preaching, were of great value to Charles. However the decisive event was the death of the minister of Holy Trinity Church. Charles had often passed by Holy Trinity and thought how wonderful it would be if he could become its minister and a herald of the gospel in the university.

At that point, Charles wrote to his father telling him of the vacancy which had occurred in Holy Trinity. His father immediately wrote to Bishop Yorke in Ely, as he had the power of presentation, meaning the power of offering the position in the church to the person of his choice. Richard Simeon knew the bishop and was friendly with him. The result was that Bishop Yorke invited Charles Simeon to become the Curate-in-Charge of Holy Trinity. This infuriated the Holy Trinity regular attenders. Although a deacon, Charles Simeon had not yet graduated. He was aged twenty-three, which was young for the position. His evangelical, biblical preaching also did not suit them. They favoured the present curate, Mr John Hammond, and wrote to Bishop Yorke. The bishop was annoyed by the letter, which he thought disrespectful, and said that even if Mr Simeon refused the offer of the office of Curate-in-Charge, it would not be offered to Mr Hammond. Charles had been thinking of declining the offer because it would mean supplanting Mr Hammond, but when he became aware of the bishop's reply, he accepted the offer.

That was not the end of Mr Hammond, however. He obviously felt aggrieved, because the congregation elected him as lecturer[5]. This entitled him to preach in Holy Trinity every Sunday at three o'clock in the afternoon and restricted Charles Simeon to the morning service.

* * *

'We'll soon sicken that Simeon fellow. He seems to think a lot of himself anyway, dressing like a toff. Did you see him going about with that umbrella? Huh, he'll be taken down a peg or two when he finds out Hammond was voted lecturer.'

'Nice guy, Mr Hammond. None of this claptrap about being born again.'

'Aye, and Simeon will see what we think of him on Sunday. The churchwardens are furious with the bishop. I reckon all the pews will be empty and locked. See how he will enjoy preaching to empty pews!'

'Do you know, I think the students will enjoy baiting him. I hear hoots and comments as he walks about Cambridge.'

'Yes, he won't last long.'

But last he did. Despite the locked pews, despite the churchwardens throwing out the chairs placed in the aisles (which he bought at his own expense), despite stones being thrown at the church windows and despite the personal abuse and attempts to disrupt

---

5. Lecturers had no duties apart from preaching and were only appointed in churches connected with universities.

the services by students, Charles Simeon showed perseverance and mildness of manner which can only be attributed to the grace of God sought in prayer and given in abundance.

This does not mean that he was a doormat. Not by any means. Students who attempted to disrupt services were openly rebuked and some even forced to make a public apology to the congregation. For despite having to stand in the aisles, bit by bit the congregation grew, attracted by his preaching. One of these students, called John Sargent, who was openly rebuked, attended the following Sunday with a changed attitude. He kept on attending and came to faith in Jesus Christ. He became a preacher and a curate to Charles Simeon.

Nevertheless, the first years of his ministry were very trying and, despite his zeal, the visits to Henry Venn at Yelling were needed times of gospel renewal and encouragement. He devised the plan to have evening services to give more scope for preaching, but this was thwarted by the churchwardens, who locked the doors. Simeon managed to get a locksmith to open the locks but decided that perseverance down that avenue was not wise. 'The servant of the Lord must not strive' (2 Timothy 2:24) was the text that kept his zealous anger in control. However, he was not one to lie down! He invited sympathetic students to his quarters on Sunday evenings instead, as a way of ministry.

* * *

Charles Simeon dragged his heels as he trudged one day in fields near Cambridge, seeking comfort. *These churchwardens, oh these churchwardens!* he exclaimed in his heart. *Will I always have them as a chain and ball dragging me down in my service of God? Now, Charles,* he chided himself, *remember that God in his wisdom has seen fit to leave them in post. Just do what God has called you to do and trust in his goodness and mercy.*

With a resigned sigh, Charles turned to his Bible. *Oh, Lord, give me a word of comfort,* he prayed in his heart. As he read in Matthew chapter 27, he came upon this verse: 'And as they came out, they found a man of Cyrene, Simon by name: him they compelled to bear his cross' (verse 32). The verse almost jumped out at him. *Simon and Simeon are just versions of the same name! Simon of Cyrene had to carry the heavy wooden cross for Jesus on his way to crucifixion on Calvary. Is it not a privilege for me to have the cross laid on me that I might carry it after Jesus? Now I can leap and sing for joy. Jesus is honouring me! No more complaining about churchwardens and unruly students — it is because of the cross of Jesus that they oppose me.*

* * *

The churchwardens might lock the doors of the church, but they could do nothing about the large quarters which Charles had in King's College. As a Fellow, Charles had the right to accommodation in King's College, and as long as he remained unmarried he could remain a Fellow. Despite his early love of dancing, for the sake of the gospel in Cambridge he remained single all his life. However, his single life was not a lonely one or an unfulfilled one.

'Come in, come in, John. Are these your friends?'

'Yes, Mr Simeon. It is their first time.'

'Welcome. I hope that John has forewarned you that I have my peculiarities. You see my lovely carpet? Well, you must brush off thoroughly the dirt of the Cambridge streets using these shoe scrapers or I shall frown at you darkly. Now I do hope that you have brought your appetites with you as we shall have a rather splendid supper.'

'We don't want to be thought gluttons, but we have heard that it is a table fit for kings,' said one student, hastily adding, 'No pun intended.'

'Ha – I appreciate your unintentional wit,' commented Charles Simeon with a smile. 'Well, I hope you students are better behaved than John was when I first made his acquaintance in Holy Trinity Church. Quite a shocker, he was.'

John Sargent reddened a little.

'Ah, but Mr Simeon, now you are a kind of hero to him and the other students ridicule him and keep calling him a Sim.'

'A Sim? What is that?'

The student looked taken aback. 'Well, ahem … Don't you know? … Well, it means that he follows your teachings.'

Charles Simeon just laughed. 'Oh, I don't suppose it is pleasant, but I can assure you I have been called a lot worse things than that. Now, after grace has been said, we will tuck into a fine supper, but I hope, too, that in the talk I will give after supper and our discussions, we will find something to feed our needy souls.

'Lord, bless the food prepared for us and those who have worked hard to provide it. All has ultimately come from our good and merciful God. Bless with a Father's blessing these good gifts and may our hearts be filled with thankfulness. Amen.'

Becoming Accepted

It was not easy for Charles Simeon to establish himself. The hostility of the churchwardens lasted for twelve years until they were replaced. Students enjoyed having a ready target for their pranks and mischief. One day, he was seen returning from church with his face and clothes plastered with dirt and rotten eggs – a trial for one so particular about his appearance. Mr Hammond was a constant niggle until he resigned after five years. Even then, Charles Simeon was not chosen as lecturer and he had to wait for another seven years before he could take up that position. Because of his devotion to prayer and frugal living he was not popular with the teaching staff. Most of the staff 'signed up' to the beliefs of the Church of England – otherwise they could not hold positions in the university – but did not take religion seriously. They must have felt uncomfortable, perhaps even exposed as hypocrites, when Charles took his faith so seriously.

Nevertheless, bit by bit he overcame prejudice and misrepresentation. Through a combination of uprightness, single-mindedness, selflessness, compassion and strictness, he won people over. He himself said, 'In this state of things I saw no remedy but faith and patience. The passage of Scripture which subdued and controlled my mind was this, "The servant of the Lord must not strive" (2 Timothy 2:24).' As a result, he did not believe it was right as a follower of Jesus to be self-assertive and demanding.

Nevertheless, students found that he could be tough and was no pushover.

Charles Randall stood sheepishly before the steady gaze of the minister of Holy Trinity Church.

'Well, young man, did you think I would do nothing? Did you think meekness would extend to accepting your outrageous behaviour during the worship of Almighty God? ... Well, did you?'

'I don't know, sir.'

'Well, I think you thought you would get off scot-free and boast to your likeminded fellows. Well, the Vice-Chancellor was highly displeased when I reported it to him. I assume he sent you here. I understand that you are to make a public apology. Now I want you to read out the apology I have prepared for you.'

'Yes, sir.'

Wearing his church gown, Charles Simeon strode into the building and stood in front of the pews. Charles Randall followed, eyes fixed on the floor.

'Before we commence divine worship, this young man has a public apology to make as ordered by the Vice-Chancellor. Step forward, Mr Randall.'

Charles Randall stepped forward and started to read in low tones. 'I, Charles Randall, confess that I –'

'Come, man, how do you expect anyone at the back to hear you? I will read out the apology for you. "I, Charles Randall, confess that I acted in a shameful and disgraceful manner when I broke one of the church windows at the beginning of divine worship and then proceeded to disrupt the service, boasting wickedly of what I had done. I apologise to the congregation of this church and its minister. I promise by the help of God never to repeat this act of desecration." Now you will sit with the congregation while I conduct the service. Also, I want to speak to you after the service.'

At the end of the service, Charles Simeon led the student into the vestry[1].

'Young man, you have suffered the humiliation of your misdeeds being made public and having an apology read out for all to hear. But I am a minister of a gospel which promises forgiveness to the sinner. However, the sinner must be sincere in seeking forgiveness. Tell me, why were you not able to read out the apology properly?'

'Mr Simeon, it is fine to act the fool with companions who then sneak away when you get into trouble, but it is

---

1. A room where a minister or others prepare for their duties and where robes are kept.

a different thing when you come on your own to make a confession. The last time I acted the fool, but this time I felt a fool.'

'That, strangely enough, was a good thing to feel. But what you did was not only foolish, it was sinful. What makes it really sinful is that you were not only mocking the God who is prepared to forgive you, but also the God who was prepared to give up his Son to the suffering of the cross to take away your sin. I beg you, I beg you seek God's forgiveness in Christ.'

Charles Randall was moved. He knew the minister he had insulted was so sincere in the appeal he had made. 'Mr Simeon, pray for me.'

Charles Simeon knelt down in the dingy vestry and the student copied him.

'Lord, we come seeking forgiveness for all our failures and folly and especially the careless way we have treated the gospel of divine mercy. Help us to see Jesus as the Lamb of God who takes away the sin of the world. Help this poor but precious sinner, Charles Randall, to repent and follow Jesus. Amen.'

The eyes of both of them were wet as they rose. From that day on, Charles Randall turned his back on his godless ways and became a staunch supporter of Charles Simeon.

Other people discovered that he was a man of spirituality and compassion. One day, when Charles was waiting to conduct a funeral, he wandered among the gravestones in the burial ground beside the church. As he did so, he observed the epitaphs written on some of the gravestones. One, in particular, caught his attention. It read:

Then from the dust of death I rise
To claim my mansion in the skies,
E'en then shall this be all my plea —
'Jesus hath liv'd and died for me'.

He at once looked round to see if there was anyone in the graveyard with whom he could share the message of the epitaph. Just then, he spotted a young woman. Her eyes were red as if she had been crying and her face was the picture of misery.

'Excuse me, dear woman, but you seem very sad. I have seen a verse on a gravestone which may help you in your distress. Come and I will show it to you.'

The woman wiped her wet cheeks and gathered her ragged skirts around her. He read the verse to her.

'That verse gives us a wonderful hope because it tells us of a wonderful Saviour. If you have that hope, all the miseries of life will be seen in a different light.'

'Oh, sir. I don't have much hope and I am certainly feeling miserable.'

'Well, now, give me your name and address and I will visit you tomorrow.'

'That is so kind of you, sir.'

The next day, Charles knocked on the door of a pitiful hovel. He was even more shocked when he was invited in. There was next to no furniture. An old grey-haired woman, wheezing with asthma, lay on a rickety bed. The woman he had met in the graveyard had a wooden crate for a seat. Two dirty children in rags tried to warm themselves at glowing cinders in a fireplace. Charles was shocked at the squalor.

'Tell me, is this your mother?'

'Yes, she is far from well. Her asthma is so bad, she can hardly speak at times.'

'Hello, I am the local minister. Don't distress yourself by trying to talk. I will try to be of assistance to your daughter.'

'Sir, I am so glad you spoke to me yesterday. I had asked my sister for help, but she turned me away. I thought there was no one to help me in this world. Now I see how foolish I was. I know there is a God who sees us in our sorrows, because he sent you into my path yesterday, sir.'

'Of that I am very glad. Now I will come back again tomorrow evening and see how I can help you. But right now we will pray.'

Kneeling down on the far-from-clean floor, he prayed till the tears flowed.

Two days later, on his third visit, he was greeted by a smile which was so different from the wretchedness in her expression in the churchyard.

'I am so glad to see you so much more cheerful,' said Charles Simeon.

'Thanks to you, sir. I have something to confess, now that the children are outside.'

'Oh, what is that?'

'Well, I will tell you what the Lord has done for me. When you called me in the churchyard, I had lain there for five hours. I thought God had utterly forsaken me and left me and my children to starve. Just when you spoke to me, I was going to drown myself. But now, sir, I am glad to say that I am trusting in the Lord.'

'Well, that gladdens my heart. I will keep in touch with you and will arrange for your children to be able to go to school.'

'Oh, sir, that would be so good. Then they might be able to get worthwhile jobs and become respectable people.'

'Well, that may be, but I pray that school will also teach them about God and the way of salvation.'

Charles valued education, but did not neglect immediate and practical help. He arranged relief for the poor during hard times. Three years after he became a minister, the winter was extremely cold. He sponsored a relief scheme during which £1,000 was subscribed. Over 7,000 people benefitted from receiving bread, coal and blankets. Three years later, there was a bread famine which badly affected the villages around Cambridge. He offered to arrange relief for them. Every Monday morning he would ride out to the villages to see for himself that the local bakers in the twenty-four villages on his list, who had received a subsidy, were being honest in selling their bread to the poor at half price as arranged. The other half of the cost was paid by himself and others whom he had asked to subscribe. He also supported the establishment of a School of Industry in Cambridge so that young people could learn practical skills which would help them get jobs. All these measures showed that he was a man of compassion and action and this contributed to his growing acceptance.

As he was not forgetful of the poor and believed that no-one is beyond the power of God to save, he visited the local jail and also preached nine times in the notorious Newgate jail in London. This, too, showed that he, like his Lord, sought out poor sinners.

He wrote to Henry Venn about a man condemned to hang for stealing a watch. Charles had been present as the man approached his execution. This, of course, was in the days when criminals condemned to hang were executed in public and were allowed to speak to the gathered crowd. *The Lord ... had given him [the condemned criminal] so strong a faith that death had entirely lost its sting; not a fear disturbed his breast. He addressed the people for near half an hour – humbling himself, exalting Christ, exhorting them to faith and repentance; and declaring the full assurance which he had of entering into glory ... After which I harangued them on the same scaffold for a few minutes on the nature of that religion which could give such serenity and joy in death. He then commended his soul into the hands of Jesus and launched into eternity without a doubt, without a sigh.*

* * *

One sign of the impact he made was when he was first asked to preach at Great St Mary's, the university church, four years after he became the minister of Holy Trinity. This was considered an honour. Before he preached, Charles went to see one of his few academic friends, Dr Glynn. He was the leading physician in Cambridge. Charles showed him the manuscript of the sermon. Dr Glynn, who was a colourful character literally, with a three-cornered hat and red cloak, suggested one or two improvements, but was very supportive. Many went that day to scoff or to distract and annoy by shuffling their feet. But, that day, the commanding presence of Charles Simeon high up in the three-tiered pulpit, the liveliness of his manner and the clarity of his presentation, silenced the congregation and riveted their attention.

Afterwards, one of the chief critics was overheard saying, 'Well, Simeon is no fool,' to which his companion replied, 'Fool! Did you ever hear such a sermon before?'

This was the first of the ten times he preached to the university. When he preached five years later, the thousand-seater church was packed and when he preached twelve years after that, many had to be turned away.

It took several years and much endurance, but Cambridge was gradually won round. When Charles was seventy-one years old and had been the minister of Trinity Church for forty-nine years, he was asked one afternoon by his friend, Joseph Gurney, how he had surmounted persecution and outlasted all the great prejudice against him in his ministry. He said to him, 'My dear brother, we must not mind a little suffering for Christ's sake. When I am getting through a hedge, if my head and shoulders are safely through, I can bear the pricking of my legs. Let us rejoice in the remembrance that our holy Head has surmounted all his suffering and triumphed over death. Let us follow him patiently; we shall soon be partakers of his victory.' His heavenly Master rewarded him with deep respect in university and church by the end of his life so that he could say at one point: *The sun and moon are scarcely more different from each other than Cambridge is from what it was when I was first minister of Trinity Church.*

Charles Simeon the Man

What kind of a man was Charles? Well, he was certainly persevering and not deterred by discouragements and blatant opposition. But he still felt the insults keenly. He was not insensitive. He talked about being 'buffeted and afflicted'.

He was disciplined, as his early rising would indicate. How many of us would get out of our beds at four o'clock and light a fire on a winter morning before spending hours reading Scripture and praying? But this was because he was stern with himself and his weaknesses. If he was late in getting up, he would discipline himself by giving a half crown to his servant – which must have delighted his servant as a half crown[1] could buy quite a bit in those days! That discipline extended to his spending. But his disciplined spending on himself was mixed with liberality towards others. This liberality only increased when he came into a big inheritance. His rule was 'to show economy to myself, liberality to my friends, and generosity to the poor.' He

---

1. Worth about £100 nowadays.

felt at home among the extremely generous evangelicals of the day who loved to do good.

He was also single-minded. Christ must have the topmost place. God was central to his thinking and living. But that did not mean that he was holed up in his study all day in an other-worldly fashion. He enjoyed and advocated physical exercise. Every day, early in the morning, he would have a swim in the River Cam. He loved horse-riding and always had good horses. Despite being frugal[2] and keeping very careful accounts of his spending, he enjoyed food and had a good appetite, so much so that jokes could be made about it.

A local person of standing called Sir Francis Chantrey was out shooting game birds one day. He achieved the amazing feat of shooting down two woodcock with one shot from one barrel. Some student wit no doubt created a few guffaws when he circulated this verse:

Let Chantrey boast his wondrous skill,
Who at one shot two cocks did kill;
This feat our Simeon's fairly beaten,
Who at one meal two cocks have eaten.

Perhaps Simeon himself would have laughed heartily at the jest about his appetite.

But his character took time to develop and he struggled with the less attractive aspects of his

---

2. Careful not to waste anything.

personality. One thing he was guilty of was extreme irritability. It led to a well-earned rebuke.

Mr Hankinson was a friend to Charles. He lived a little distance from Cambridge and Charles had ridden to spend an hour or so with him. Mr Hankinson had left the room to instruct the cook to bring tea and sweet baking. Meanwhile, a servant was in front of the fire, stoking it with a long brass poker. Charles, who was still chilled from the ride, grew more and more irritated as the man kept poking at the fire.

Grabbing a paper and rolling it up, he whacked the man on the back. 'Begone! Why are you poking that fire to death.'

The astonished servant mumbled, 'I'm sorry, sir,' and rushed off.

'Your servant is terribly annoying,' complained Charles when his friend returned. 'He nearly poked that fire to death.'

'Oh,' replied Mr Hankinson, with raised eyebrows. 'He is nevertheless a good servant.'

When the afternoon was over, Charles called for his horse, which had been left to graze. The servant appeared with the horse. Charles and his friend went out. The servant nervously struggled to put on the bridle and the horse, not used to him, stamped a hoof and whinnied.

'Give me that bridle!' yelled Charles. 'Can't you do anything right?' Pale and shocked, the servant scurried away.

'Charles, you attach the bridle and get the horse ready. I have to do something in the house which will not take a minute.'

Five minutes later, Mr Hankinson returned and, unseen by the fuming Charles, slipped a letter into Charles's bag.

Now ready, Charles mounted, his face still red and angry. 'If I were you, I'd get rid of that useless fellow.' Still incensed, off he rode.

When he reached his quarters and his ill-humour had subsided, he discovered the note which his friend had written, but which was written as if from the servant. The following struck home to Charles's conscience: 'I do not see how a man who preached and prayed so well could be in such a passion about nothing and wear no bridle on his tongue.' It was signed 'John Softly'. The result was that Charles wrote the following letter to the servant: 'To John Softly, from Charles, Proud and Irritable. I most cordially thank you, my dear friend, for your kind and seasonable reproof.' Then he wrote to his friend Mr Hankinson: 'I hope, my dearest brother, that when you find your soul nigh[3] to God, you will remember who so greatly needs all the help he can get.' That one, obviously, was Charles Simeon!

Although that episode shows that he could fly off the handle, it also shows that he could be humble and contrite. He did not bear grudges. Daniel Corrie, who became a bishop in India, told the following story:

---

3. Near.

*It occurred when I was almost a freshman [a first year student].
On returning one evening after a Thursday evening service to
Mrs Dornford's in Pease Hill, I was asked by a junior member
of the family what I thought of Mr Simeon's sermon. I replied it
was too long by half; little thinking that my questioner would
observe to Mr Simeon, 'What do you think this boy says of your
sermon?' Mr Simeon pretended not to hear the remark, but on
it being repeated, replied, 'The boy is right; I felt it so myself.'*
[This has been adapted.]

He was also realistic about himself and often
bitterly regretted his sinfulness. He once said, 'I love
the valley of humiliation. I there feel that I am in
my proper place.' So, although he could flare up, he
was generally a wise and peaceable person. He was a
moderate, not an extremist. There was a very significant
encounter between him and John Wesley, the leader of
the Methodist movement. John Wesley had views he
could not agree with, such as that Christians could fall
away and be lost. But Charles cleverly found a way of
disarming conflict.

'Well, Mr Wesley, I suppose you and I should be at
loggerheads[4]. But let me ask you some questions. Do
you feel yourself such a sinful creature that you would
not have thought of turning to God if God had not first
put it in your heart?'

'Yes, I do indeed.'

'And do you utterly despair of recommending
yourself to God by anything you do but rather look

---

4. In serious disagreement.

for salvation through the blood and righteousness of Jesus?'

'Yes, solely through Christ.'

'But, sir, supposing you were first saved by Christ, are you not somehow or other to save yourself afterwards by your own good works?'

'No. I must be saved by Christ from first to last.'

'Allowing, then, that you were first turned by the grace of God, are you not in some way or other to keep yourself by your own power?'

'No.'

'What, then, are you to be upheld every hour and every moment by God, as much as an infant in its mother's arms?'

'Yes, altogether.'

'And is all your hope in the grace and mercy of God to preserve you unto his heavenly kingdom?'

'Yes, I have no hope but in him.'

'Then I have no quarrel with you in these matters, Mr Wesley.'

* * *

He was very conscientious, too. This applied not only to time and money, but especially to his responsibility to preach the gospel. He did not shirk to paint sin in its true colours or warn people about their spiritual danger. Ministerial faithfulness was a priority. He did not pander[5] to his hearers, as vividly illustrated by one time he was preaching.

---

5. Please by saying what they want to hear.

Simeon gazed round the crowded church as he paused significantly in his address.

'You see,' his voice resounded through the church, 'a minister is like the keeper of a lighthouse set on a craggy coastline. That keeper's responsibility is to keep the lights shining to warn of the dangers of that rocky coastline, which would tear to splinters the wooden hull of any ship run aground on them.

But one day when a strong north-easterly wind built up a powerful swell and just as darkness descended, that light-keeper fell asleep. As the first streaks of pink were appearing in the clouds the next morning, he awoke with a jerk. The light! It was out! He shot up to the light and managed to get it started. The beams once more flashed out over the watery waste.

But when he looked out on the heaving sea, what did he see? A scene of horror – broken spars, a battered vessel, torn and flapping sails, a smashed dinghy and, worst of all, corpses floating on the grey sea or scattered among the debris on the shore.

Already, as the daylight increased, companies of people made their way to the shore. Their loud wailing froze the blood in the veins of the lighthouse keeper. He made his way down to the shore.

What happened? Why did they end up on the rocks when there is a lighthouse to warn them?

The lighthouse keeper's face reddened. "They did not see the rocks. The light was out."

"Out! How did it go out?"

"I was asleep."

"Asleep! Asleep!" yelled the bereft, anguished crowd.

And if ever I fail to warn of the danger of eternal lostness for those who refuse Christ as Saviour and if ever I fail to preach the need to be born again, shame me with that cry, "Asleep! Asleep!"'

The power of that sermon was one which people spoke about for years.

This sense of responsibility was both spiritual and social. This, combined with a talent for organisation, led him to organise his parish into small areas for visiting. He called this a 'Visiting Society'. Each district had a male and female church member responsible for finding out who were in distress through poverty or illness and giving those they visited spiritual help. Once a month, the visitors would meet together and report to Charles on what they had done. This helped Charles be aware of the need in his parish and also gave ordinary church members the opportunity to have an active role.

* * *

As a minister, especially when he became accepted and his reputation steadily grew, he was asked for advice and as a result did much letter-writing. In this, as in many aspects of his ministry, he showed great wisdom. Sometimes he would set out good principles:

'I should be cautious about making up my mind *strongly* on anything that is not clearly defined in Scripture.'

When a person becomes celebrated and one's opinions are eagerly sought, it is easy to become big-headed. The opposite happened with Charles. He was seen as self-important and vain in his early years as a preacher. Through hard trials and self-knowledge gained over time, he would later write: *I love simplicity; I love contrition[6]. Even religion itself I do not love if it be not cast in a mould of humility.*

Supremely, however, he loved Christ. He was passionate about the gospel. God absorbed his soul. Samuel Marsden witnessed this when he visited Charles's quarters one day. Samuel was thickset and fresh-faced, having worked on his father's farm in Yorkshire before becoming a preacher. Now, he was studying for ordination as a minister. He was being encouraged by Charles to prepare for missionary service abroad. Needing reassurance and spiritual guidance, he thought he would call on his mentor.

Samuel was careful to scrape the yellow dust of the Cambridge streets off his shoes. As he was about to knock on the heavy oak door, he heard the low sound of Charles Simeon's voice. Did he already have a visitor? But he could hear no other voice. He pushed the door open so that he could peep in. There was Charles Simeon kneeling over his Bible at his devotions. As he gazed at his minister and friend, he heard him burst out with the words, 'Glory! Glory!' oblivious to the fact that someone had come in.

---

6. Deep sorrow for wrongdoing.

His Band of Brothers

In time, after the initial surge of hostility had subsided and he had gathered a faithful few around him, Charles started prayer and Bible study with them on Friday evenings in a hired room in the parish. It was not long until he had built up support and the hired room was too small. He then hired rooms outside his own parish to conduct evening worship and teach his flock. This was irregular, and might have landed him in trouble with other ministers, but no objections were ever made to him by the minister of the parish.

As his ministry started to stretch out, so Charles Simeon developed as a preacher. Strange as it may seem, preachers in the Church of England were not taught to preach. The university taught them Greek and Hebrew and Philosophy[1] among other things, but it did not teach them how to construct a sermon which would convey Bible truth effectively or deliver it in a way which kept the attention of the listeners. So, in many ways, he was self-taught as a preacher. That did not mean, however,

---

1. The study of the nature of reality, existence and knowledge.

that he thought aspiring ministers should not be taught the principles of making and preaching a sermon.

No doubt, Charles's early curates or assistants, such as John Sargent, were given many helpful instructions and friendly criticisms. Classes of instruction in preaching started eight years after he became a minister. Stemming from Simeon's commitment to preaching the gospel to the people of Cambridge was a commitment to training young men for gospel ministry. He gathered a small group of men into his rooms twice a month to explain his views on preaching. Then, one of them would preach a sermon that he had prepared and Simeon would give feedback. Charles felt that this was a real responsibility as part of his calling: 'I have, as my work, undertaken to provide ministers for eternal souls.' However, he was not satisfied. After twenty years in Holy Trinity when he moved his rooms, he started holding what he called 'Conversation Classes'. The purpose of the 'Conversation Classes' was to encourage and instruct young men in the work of the ministry and in what was required in preaching the gospel.

These were held in his accommodation high up in Gibb's Building which was very roomy compared with his first quarters there. One large bay window overlooked the River Cam and the bay window on the other side of the main room overlooked the courtyard, which separated the college from Cambridge itself. (There was access to the roof and Charles often used to go there to gaze down on his parish and pray.)

* * *

The conversation class was buzzing with chatter. As each new student arrived, Charles, with faultless manners, would smile, bow and stretch out his hand in welcome. Charles was now silvery-haired and a recognised Christian leader.

Centrepiece on the grand mahogany table was the minster's precious black Wedgwood teapot (this teapot is still preserved in the vestry of Holy Trinity). Though careful with his spending, he could appreciate fine things. Two servants poured out cups of tea and distributed them to the assembled young men. Tea was still expensive in those times.

'Now, friends, I rejoice to see you all assembled. There was a day, nearly thirty years ago, when I could not have attracted a gathering like this supposing I paid each of you £500 to attend. Now I love these little conversation meetings. They spread a spirit of love among us. They seem a foretaste of heaven. Well, let us begin.'

Charles took his seat. It was a substantial chair set up higher than the others. He rested his hands on his knees.

'The subject for the evening is preparation for preaching. Now remember, before a sermon is prepared, the preacher must be prepared – prepared in his heart. For a sermon with no heart and soul behind it, is a feeble thing. Preaching is declaring the astonishing grace of God in Jesus Christ and deserves to be vigorously proclaimed. So …'

After twenty minutes of wise advice, Charles paused and smiled encouragingly. 'Now, friends, you have heard enough for our conversation to start. If you have any questions to ask, I shall be happy to hear them and give what assistance I can.'

'Mr Simeon, aren't there times when a preacher feels so inadequate and yet you have set a high standard?'

'Thank you for your question. A preacher should always feel inadequate. The Apostle Paul tells us that we are clay jars – but these jars contain the excellency of the gospel. But if we think too much upon our inadequacies, we will be discouraged. Don't look at the fragile clay. Think about the excellencies of the gospel. Think about the excellencies of Jesus Christ. As you do so, your hearts should glow and your sermons catch fire. Does that answer your question?'

'Yes, indeed.'

And so, the questions and observations and discussion went on.

These times of fellowship and learning in Charles's room built up a strong bond between Charles and those who attended. They became a band of brothers. Although for the first fourteen years he ministered alone, when Charles grew in popularity he employed curates, sometimes as many as three at one time. When he became lecturer, he often asked the curate to take the lecture while he went to minister in some outlying village in the area surrounding Cambridge.

One of the curates who became a special friend to him was Thomas Thomason. He was a curate to Charles for twelve years. He became curate at Stapleford outside Cambridge and lived in a former manor in the adjoining village of Shelford. Because it was so spacious, conferences for spiritual growth and fellowship were organised yearly both for men and for women. Thomas Thomason had a room prepared for Charles which was like a little retreat for him to come and meditate undisturbed. Most of the people in the Stapleford area were very poor, so Charles at his own expense established a small factory for making rope, which proved very successful and provided employment. Thomas Thomason eventually went as a missionary to India and established an orphanage there.

Charles had a passion not only for preaching but for all gospel outreach and instruction.

One day, a small group stood outside Holy Trinity after morning worship.

'That was a great sermon about being light and salt. He was on fire today.'

'Yes, he is a rousing preacher, isn't he?'

'Now listen here, you gownsmen, what use is it standing here applauding the sermon and doing nothing? We need to stop talking and do something to spread the light,' said a Mr Wright.

There was an embarrassed silence. 'Well, what do you propose we do?'

'Well, we could go to one of the nearby villages and see if we can do anything to teach the children.'

The students looked at each other. 'Okay,' said one student, 'I have been out at Bardwell and I doubt if the children receive much gospel teaching there.'

'Okay, then,' said Mr Wright, 'I will have a word with Mr Simeon and see what he says.'

The result was that they went to Bardwell to see if the children would come to Cambridge if classes were organised. It was an immediate success. Two hundred and twenty children arrived on the doorstep of the Friends' Meeting House in Jesus Lane on the opening day. They were divided into twenty-six classes and the instruction was effective and popular. It was an ideal field of training for future ministers. When the organisers wanted to open up other branches, Charles said, 'Put your hand in my pocket when you want anything.' Over the years, no less than sixty of its former teachers went out as missionaries with the Church Missionary Society.

A Friend in Persia

John Sargent looked at the slight figure of Henry Martyn as he approached. 'Well, Mr Martyn, I have been noticing you in church these days. Are you enjoying the services?'

'I have to confess that I am enjoying them much more than I used to – not that there was anything wrong with Mr Simeon's preaching in the past, I hasten to add.'

'Oh! What has made the difference, then? Would you like to come along to my room in the college? We can chat as we go along.'

'That is very kind of you. To answer your question, I remember my sister writing me to urge me to read my Bible and pray and seek the Lord, but it only seemed to irritate me.'

'I am afraid, Mr Martyn, that I, too, scorned good advice and "kicked over the traces"[1] when I came here first.' They strode along the narrow dusty Cambridge streets oblivious to the curious glances of townsfolk and the colourful swirling

---

1. Rebelled.

gowns of undergraduates and fellows. 'But carry on with your story.'

'My father was a godly believer. He started as a miner and by hard work became a mining agent. I admired my father, so his death, while I was in Cambridge a year ago, devastated me. However, I knew he was in heaven, but where would I be if I suddenly died? I couldn't get his example and my sister's urgings out of my mind. Gradually, I came to see the light of Christ and came to a living faith.'

'Here we are now. Do come in. My room isn't spacious, but it is quite comfortable. I will make some tea, to which I am very partial.' John Sargent filled the kettle and set it on the lit stove. 'I was interested in your story. I often find that some act of providence[2] such as your father's death initiates a spiritual change. So what do you intend to prepare yourself for after your studies?'

'Well, Mr Sargent, I have been thinking about pursuing a career in law. It is an honourable one.'

'I have been hearing that you are a brilliant student and recently announced Senior Wrangler [top student in mathematics].'

A pink glow flushed Henry Martyn's thin cheeks and he looked down modestly at his shoes. 'I enjoy study, sir.'

John Sargent sat tapping his fingers together thoughtfully. 'Now tell me, have you ever thought of the Christian ministry?'

---

2. God's ordering of the world and the events of life.

Henry Martyn started. 'What! Become a minister? But I am such a young Christian.'

John Sargent laughed. 'I hope I did not shock you too much. What you say is true. You are yet a child in the faith – but some children grow quickly. I feel that the Lord has given you talents and that these talents should be at his disposal. I am of the opinion that you would find a chat with Mr Simeon very helpful.'

'Mr Simeon!' spluttered Henry.

'He is very approachable despite what you might think and loves helping students. Now before I worry you more, would you like a cup of tea?'

'That would be most welcome. Does tea have a calming effect?'

John Sargent laughed again. 'I think it will in your case.'

* * *

'Come in!' boomed Charles Simeon when he heard a timid knock at the door. In stepped a young man with narrow features and slightly curly, dark hair. 'Ah, Henry Martyn. Now did you wipe your feet properly at the outer door?'

'Yes, sir, I did.'

'Ah, you have been well warned about my little obsessions then. I gather that you have had a chat with John Sargent, my brother minister. I am glad you have come. Please sit down.'

Charles looked straight at his guest. 'Now, Mr Martyn, I always like to be direct, without being rude.

John Sargent suggested that you might make a good minister. What do you think?'

'Mr Sargent threw me into confusion. I was thinking of a lucrative[3] profession such as the law.'

'And are you still thinking of a lucrative profession?'

'Being rich means nothing to me. My father started poor but did well in life, yet never put wealth or position before his God. I know that choosing to serve God in the church will mean that I will never be rich.'

'Well said. You have recently become Senior Wrangler and people are full of admiration for your achievement. Do you think that will continue if you were to become a minister?'

'Jesus never sought popularity and often required silence from those he had cured. Besides, I hear that you yourself, sir, battled on through unpopularity with your eyes only on the praise of God.'

A broad smile crossed Charles's face. 'An even better answer. I am warming to you, Henry. Another question: what would be the greatest obstacle in your mind to becoming a minister?'

Henry Martyn thought for a moment. 'I think it would be the thought of unfitness, the thought that I would be useless and barren without anything to show at the end of my ministry.'

'I see. A final question. Do you think it a greater honour to preach the gospel or to be a lawyer in a courtroom?'

---

3. Producing much financial gain.

'There is only one possible answer. To preach the gospel is greater than to be a top lawyer.'

'Well, Henry, I love your frankness and think we need to meet again. In my view, John Sargent was right and I urge you to think seriously about devoting yourself to the Christian ministry. I will pray for you earnestly.'

'Thank you, sir. You are so kind.'

* * *

A deep friendship grew between Charles and Henry Martyn. Henry's academic career flourished. A year after becoming Senior Wrangler, he won the Latin prize and became a Fellow of St John's College. Henry studied for holy orders and was ordained a deacon in 1803. As a measure of his respect and fondness for Henry Martyn, Charles Simeon asked him to join Thomas Thomason as a curate on his staff. Thomas Thomason was curate at Shelford, about five miles from Cambridge, and Henry Martyn was given special responsibility for the village of Loworth, six miles from Cambridge.

Henry Martyn's name is not remembered today, however, for his work in Loworth. He is famed as a missionary of intense devotion and self-sacrifice who died young in his mission to bring the Scriptures to India and Persia. This intensity is seen in one of his diary entries when he arrived in India: 'Now let me burn out for God.'

How did that happen? One influence was the life and diary of David Brainerd, missionary to the

American Indians. Brainerd, too, was intense and self-sacrificing in order to bring good news to the lost. The other influence was a powerful sermon by Charles Simeon drawing attention to the life and work of William Carey, the Baptist missionary to India. Charles and Henry's friendship spurred each other on to serve the Lord.

* * *

The harnesses jangled and the hooves clattered as Charles and Henry rode from Cambridge to join up with Thomas Thomason.

'Now, Henry, I believe you have been having serious thoughts of going to India. I am pleased to think that I have been instrumental in directing your thoughts to that needy part of the world.'

'Mr Simeon, your description of the courage and vision and tenacity of William Carey destroyed any petty ambitions I may have had and set a love for the people of India burning in my heart.'

'You realise, of course, that there are immense barriers which exist – language, ingrained religious ideas and practices, resentment of foreigners, serpents, tigers and diseases not encountered in this land.'

'I am prepared. One of my heroes is David Brainerd, and he did not flinch from discouragement or illness or danger or misunderstanding.'

'It is a hot day. Let us draw up at this trough to water the horses.'

While the horses drank, both men thought about India.

'Do you know anyone who has been to India, Henry?'

'No, Mr Simeon. Do you?'

'I know some who have gone as chaplains and missionaries and who write to me – David Brown for instance. I may show you some of his letters to give you insight.'

'I would appreciate that.'

'I have heard that some obstacles have arisen to your going to India.'

'That is true. My father left my sister and I provided for, but an unforeseen financial problem means that our means of support have been removed. I feel responsible for my sister.'

'I am sorry about that, Henry, for I am sure your father thought he was providing wisely. I do not think all is lost, however. I have good contacts with the East India Company, who will listen to my advice on the appointment of chaplains. It may well be that you could go to India with sufficient a salary to support your sister.'

'I was trusting that the Lord would open up a way. If you are able to make these contacts and arrange a chaplainship, my heart would overflow with gratitude to you and the Lord.'

'Well, let us get on our way or Thomas will be wondering what has become of us.'

* * *

True to his word, Charles wrote to William Wilberforce, the slave trade abolitionist and MP and Charles Grant, MP and member of the Board of the East India Company, with a letter of introduction. Henry was introduced to the Board, who received the recommendation favourably. However, he had to wait until he was twenty-four and ordained to the ministry. He preached his farewell sermon on 2nd April, 1805 in Holy Trinity Church on the text: 'For Thou, O LORD of hosts, God of Israel, hast revealed to thy servant, saying, I will build thee an house: therefore hath thy servant found in his heart to pray this prayer unto thee. And now, O Lord GOD, thou art that God, and thy words be true, and thou hast promised this goodness unto thy servant: Therefore now let it please thee to bless the house of thy servant, that it may continue for ever before thee: for thou, O Lord GOD, hast spoken it: and with thy blessing let the house of thy servant be blessed for ever' (2 Samuel 7:27-29).

When in Portsmouth on board the ship *Union*, waiting to sail, he was visited by Charles Simeon and was given a gift from the Holy Trinity Church of a silver compass, which greatly touched him. He wrote thanking them and pleading for prayer. 'Pray not only for my soul - that I may be kept faithful unto death - but also specially for the souls of the poor heathen.'

But that was not the end of the Simeon-Martyn connection. Henry had fallen in love with the refined and beautiful Miss Lydia Grenfell. Even before he sailed they had met together. Lydia was not a forceful character but her mother was! She did not want Henry as a son-in-law. Despite her opposition, Henry proposed to Lydia by letter three months after arriving in India. He asked Charles Simeon to try to persuade her. Charles made the long trip to Cornwall in response, but all his persuasive powers failed to make the desired impact. Eight months after receiving the letter, Lydia wrote rejecting Henry's proposal of marriage. Despite the disappointment, Henry still kept in touch with her by letter.

Shortly before he left India to go to Persia, in 1810, to further his translation of the Bible into Persian, Henry Martyn had his portrait painted and sent to England as a gift to Charles Simeon. Two years later, he was dead due to overwork and the lung disease tuberculosis, known then as consumption. Charles used to comment on Henry Martyn's picture, while looking up at it with affectionate earnestness, as it hung over his fireplace, 'There! see that blessed man! What an expression of countenance[4]! No one looks at me as he does - he never takes his eyes off one; and seems always to be saying, "Be serious – oh don't trifle – don't trifle."' Then smiling at the picture he would add, 'And I won't trifle – I won't trifle.' Later, Charles bequeathed the portrait to the University of Cambridge. Without his prompting, encouragement and practical arrangements, would one of the most inspirational of mission stories have occurred at all or such a tragic-heroic figure be remembered?

---

4. Face.

The Clapham Sect

Nowadays, a sect is thought of as a cult characterised by false teaching. That certainly was not true of the group, within the Church of England in the late eighteenth century and early nineteenth century, known as the Clapham Sect. They were loyal to the Church of England and faithful to its teachings.

How did they come to be recognised as different? Well, Clapham, at the end of the eighteenth century was a prosperous village outside London, south of the Thames. John Venn, son of Henry Venn, who was an early spiritual mentor to Charles, became Rector of Holy Trinity Church, Clapham in 1792 and served there until his death in 1813. John Venn and Charles Simeon had been good friends in Cambridge, once Charles had been introduced to him. Clapham had become a centre for evangelical and philanthropic[1] action even before John Venn arrived, but he strongly supported evangelicals who

---

1. Helping the needy and deprived.

had a social conscience. Their idealism and religious zeal gave rise to the nickname 'The Saints'. It was given to them by those who resented a religion which preached evangelical conversion[2]. They also resented that 'The Saints' challenged practices which caused poor people to suffer, for example: children being sent up chimneys to remove soot. The name Clapham Sect was given to them later and the label stuck. Some of its members attended the Eclectic Society, a Christian discussion group, formed in 1783, one of whose members was John Newton of 'Amazing Grace' fame[3]. Charles Simeon had strong connections with the Clapham Sect. The connection started in his early twenties – shortly after he was brought to faith and not yet a minister – when a letter arrived at his door ...

'Ah, what is this? A letter? Who is it from, I wonder? I do not recognise the handwriting.'

Carefully, Charles broke the red wax seal – he was always very particular, even fussy – and opened the letter, which was written on high quality woven paper. He sat and read it slowly.

---

2. Turning to God and turning away from a life of sin in response to the good news of Jesus Christ.

3. John Newton was a Church of England minister who at one time had lived far from God and been a slave trader. The hymn 'Amazing Grace' was written to praise God for his mercy to him. Its first lines are:

Amazing grace, how sweet the sound

That saved a wretch like me.

Dear Mr Simeon

You may never have heard of me, and in that I will have the advantage of you. My name is John Thornton. I am well known to Mr Venn, Rector at Yelling, and to others who have informed me of your faith and determination to serve the Lord in the ministry of the gospel. I have quite an extensive number of Christian friends and seek to do good practically and spiritually when and where I can. If I can help in practical matters, do not hesitate to contact me.

As you are yet pursuing your studies, some advice from me will not go amiss. Watch continually over your own spirit and do all in love; we must grow downwards in humility to soar heavenward. I hope you will receive this advice in the right spirit and that a valued friendship may result.

A fellow servant of Jesus Christ,

John Thornton

'Hmm, he's right, I have never heard of him. But the advice is good. He seems to be somebody of influence. I had better ask Mr Venn next time I venture out to Yelling. In fact, it is a good excuse for going there tomorrow!'

After Charles's ride to Yelling the following day, he was greeted warmly by his old friend, Henry Venn.

'Come in, come in, Charles. Hang up your greatcoat on that hook. I heard your horse before I saw you and was wondering who it was. You have such a lovely horse and go at a good canter.'

'Yes, I love to ride and relish the fresh air of the countryside.'

'So, Charles, I think something unusual must have brought you here. This is not your usual visiting time.'

'You are as observant as ever, Mr Venn. I received a letter yesterday from a gentleman I have no personal knowledge of. He revealed only sparse information about himself. I wondered if you may be able to enlighten me.'

'Ah! So, who is this gentleman? Do you have this letter with you?'

Charles took out the letter from a large inner pocket in his greatcoat and passed it over to Mr Venn.

'It is from my friend Mr Thornton. Now, Charles, Mr Thornton is a fine Christian who has a love for the Lord and for people. He is a wealthy man, having been a merchant.'

'He seems to be very generous.'

'Wonderfully so.'

'So how do you know him?'

'When I was younger and before I became Vicar in Huddersfield, I was a curate in Clapham. John Thornton belongs to Clapham. We have corresponded ever since.'

'I am very privileged to have come to his attention, then.'

'I am afraid, Charles, that I have a confession to make. I wrote to him and drew his attention to you.'

'Oh, Mr Venn, you have nothing to apologise for. I would be honoured to have a friendly correspondence with him.'

'I think it would be good for you to get to know his son, Henry, too. Henry is a banker and a young man with ambitions to be an MP. He has problems, though, as he will not bribe people to vote for him.'

'An upright person, I see. Just the kind we need in parliament.'

'Now, Charles, you have ridden over from Cambridge and must be in need of something to keep you going. Will you stay for lunch? My daughters would be pleased to have your company.'

'You are very hospitable.'

* * *

The link with Clapham was strengthened when John Venn became rector there. Quite a number of the Clapham Sect had been to Cambridge University and come under the influence of Charles Simeon. Just as he himself had been encouraged by letters from John Thornton and Rev John Newton, the evangelical leader and hymn writer, he advised young men and he encouraged them to join in practical Christian action, along with others associated with Clapham.

So, what practical things did the Clapham Sect do or campaign for? The list is impressive: they agitated for improved education, the abolition of press gangs as a means of recruiting sailors for the navy, improvements to the penal code[4] and reform of parliament and the voting system among other things. Wilberforce even set up the first charity to prevent cruelty to animals.

---

4. The laws governing the punishment of people who break the law.

They supported charitable initiatives and were very generous to good causes.

However, their greatest focus was the abolition of the slave trade and, when that was achieved, the abolition of slavery itself. This was not a one-man campaign. There were very important contributions made by John Newton, Henry Venn, Thomas Clarkson, James Stephen and Thomas Fowell Buxton. But the one who spearheaded the campaign in parliament tirelessly and was a brilliant advocate of abolition, was William Wilberforce – who was a cousin of Henry Thornton, the MP and banker. His life's work saw its fulfilment three days before he died when the bill abolishing slavery was finally accepted.

William Wilberforce was not brought to faith through Charles Simeon. That distinction belonged to another Cambridge man, Rev. Isaac Milner, who was a keen supporter of the Clapham Sect and brilliant mathematician and experimenter.

Isaac Milner and Charles Simeon shared a devotion to Cambridge University and a love for the debates held by the Eclectic Society of the Clapham Sect.

* * *

Isaac Milner heaved his great bulk down from his carriage. He was weary from his long journey from London but brightened up when he saw the dapper figure of Charles Simeon approach, sporting his trademark umbrella.

'I say, Charles, your immaculate appearance makes me feel like a bit of a tramp after the mud and puddles of the London road.'

'Well, Isaac, a quick change and I am sure you will be thoroughly presentable. It is a wearisome journey, but I am sure, too, that your fellowship in London at the Eclectic Society will have left you energised in spirit.'

'Yes, we had a real time of strengthening of the weary hands. I am always amazed at the energy these people have to pursue good causes.'

'That's true. I am sorry that I was not able to be present. Was there a good number there?'

'Oh, yes. But many were asking for you and regretting your absence. The way the work has progressed here in Cambridge, both at King's and now at Queens' since I came back as President, has really encouraged them.'

'I must make an effort to be at the next gathering. I often write to encourage William in his anti-slave trade drive, but speaking face-to-face is so much better.'

'Yes, Charles, William was disappointed that you were not there. He said that you refresh his soul and make him want to live closer to the Lord. He is such a gift to us, such a wonderful speaker and so persevering in the face of setbacks.'

'Yes, Isaac, I am sure that he has been raised up for such a day as this and will see the end of this shameful enslavement of our fellow men. Let us continue to uphold him mightily in prayer.'

'Well said, Charles. I will go for that quick change now. The Lord bless you.'

'And you, too, my learned friend.'

* * *

Charles Simeon's visits to the Eclectic Society were indeed precious times of encouragement and strengthening. After one of these gatherings of like-minded evangelical activists, William Wilberforce in his diary wrote: Simeon with us – his heart glowing with love of Christ. How full he is of love, and of desire to promote the spiritual benefit of others. Oh! that I might copy him as he Christ.

Mission to the World

Charles Simeon encouraged many young men, including some of his curates, to offer themselves for Christian service overseas, especially in India. Henry Martyn may have been the most famous of them, but he was only one of a large number. It is true that Charles only sent out one missionary – who worked for fifteen years in Syria and Palestine – but this is because in India missionaries were severely restricted by the East India Company, who acted as if they were the rulers. An example is the famous Baptist pioneer missionary, William Carey, who was forced by the East India Company to restrict himself to a Danish settlement at Serampore. Instead, Charles cultivated relationships with officials in the East India Company to send out chaplains to India. They could freely learn the local languages and translate the Scriptures without interference. Charles's commitment to missionary friends meant that once he even accompanied a friend on the first stage of his journey to India.

* * *

Charles Simeon and Thomas Thomason, stood on the deck of the sailing ship *Travers*, an East Indiaman[1], looking out over the waves of the English Channel as the ship pulled away from the Isle of Wight.

'Mr Simeon, I can't say how comforting it was to have you come to see me off – and now you are sailing down the channel with me!'

'Thomas, I owe you so much. You were so good when I was ill last year and could scarcely preach at all. I was more like one dead than alive. You bore the burden of preaching and overseeing so uncomplainingly! We have been such spiritual brothers, that showing my oneness with you by going down the channel a little is no hardship.'

'Brothers? More like father and son, I think,' laughed Thomas.

'So, my son, how will you occupy yourself during the tedious voyage ahead?'

'I intend to study hard at learning Persian. I have already learned some Arabic and Hindu.'

'That was what dear Henry Martyn did on his voyage, too.'

'Pray for me and pray for my dear wife, Elizabeth. She is not only reconciled to going to India but firmly believes that she should embrace it as God's will. But it will try her strength and resolve.'

---

1. A sailing ship licensed by the East India Company to carry cargo and passengers to and from territories it controlled.

'As God enables me, I shall pray daily for both of you. It is a dangerous voyage and you go to a land of strange illnesses and dark spiritual forces. Shall we stroll further along the deck?'

* * *

Charles certainly spoke true, for the journey which began on 10th June, 1808 nearly ended in tragedy on 7th November when the *Travers* hit rocks and in a short time had broken up. Most, apart from 16, escaped: 91 on an overloaded longboat, 18 on a cutter and 11 on a smaller boat, but they had to endure rough seas and violent squalls for three and a half hours before being rescued by other ships. All the Thomason family escaped, but only a handful of small but prized possessions was salvaged.

* * *

Charles Simeon never became a bishop with spiritual authority over an area called a diocese, but he jokingly wrote: 'I used ... to call India my diocese. Since there has been a bishop I modestly call it my province[2].'

By this he meant that when the Church of England appointed a bishop to Calcutta in India in 1814, India became that bishop's diocese, so Charles could no longer refer humorously to India as his diocese. In fact, one of his own protégés[3], Daniel Corrie, in 1835 became the first Bishop of Madras in India. Even later, he was very friendly with Bishop Daniel Wilson of Calcutta,

---

2. An area of a larger country which has its own identity and governing body e.g the provinces of Quebec and Ontario in Canada.

3. People helped and supported by older, experienced people.

appointed in 1832. Simeon was not a traveller and only twice visited the Netherlands and Paris, but despite the fact he was never in India, his impact was significant.

* * *

Charles settled down on the beautifully upholstered settee with carved mahogany legs and beamed at William Wilberforce.

'Congratulations, William. The Charter Bill has been passed by Parliament. A bishopric in Calcutta![4] Amazing! It has been a huge struggle to free things up and get India opened to mission.'

'Yes, indeed. Taking on the might of the East India Company and its supporters in Parliament is no light task. But recently their power grabs and arrogance have created enemies. Their day will come.'

'I think back twenty-six years ago to 1787, when I received a letter from that dear minister of God and sincere friend, David Brown. The heartfelt, pleading tone in that letter started my spiritual love for India. Not that my efforts at the time were successful.'

'Ha! Charles, that must have been a trial to you. You aren't the world's most patient minister.'

'I am of an impetuous[5] temperament, I freely admit, and patience is something I am slowly learning.'

'Well, your impatience is the result of a keenness to see progress and real achievement in the Lord's work

---

4. A bishopric is the area under the control of a bishop. Calcutta is a large city in India.

5. Acting quickly without thought or care.

and I can't fault that. Why, you have spurred me on many a time by your zeal.'

'You are very kind to say that, William. I sometimes rub people up the wrong way.'

'Well, there are plenty of MPs in the House of Commons whom I rub up the wrong way. Many would love it if I were struck dumb. But perseverance in the face of opposition led to the abolition of the slave trade in the dominions[6] and now perseverance in the face of opposition has led to missionary freedom.'

'Keep going, William. You have much work to do yet.'

'I know, but today is a day for rejoicing in a large brick being taken out of the dam wall. Let us pray that the trickle will become a flood.'

'Your eloquence, William, is a gift from God, and I am glad that you are using it for God. I just pray, too, that the freedom for missionary enterprise in the territories controlled by the East India Company, will bring gospel freedom to those shackled by superstition and false religion. Let's give thanks to God now.'

* * *

On 16th February 1799, the Eclectic Society gathered in the vestry of St John's Chapel, Bedford Road, London.

There was a shuffling of feet, a low hum of conversation and a clearing of clerical throats as the Rev John Venn, Chairman of the Society, rose to his feet. Silence fell and all eyes were on him. There was

---

6. The lands ruled in the empire.

an expectant, charged atmosphere which was almost palpable[7].'

'Gentlemen, we thank God that we are blessed to meet again as a Society. As you know, our topic today is one much-discussed among us: "With what propriety[8] and in what mode can a mission be attempted to the heathen from the established church?" Mr Charles Grant has a proposal to make.'

Charles Grant, one of those who first interested Charles Simeon in India, got to his feet. 'Gentlemen, like you, I believe in the propriety of mission to the heathen. I also believe in the propriety of the Church of England engaging in such mission. But my experience with the East India Company leads me to think that the authorities will be much more favourable if those sent out are well-trained and qualified. My proposal is to campaign for the establishment of a missionary seminary to train missionaries. Good, well-trained missionaries could prove that the fears of the authorities are unfounded.'

'Well, Mr Grant, you have made your suggestion. I now ask Charles Simeon to speak to us. His passion for mission to the heathen is known throughout the church.'

Charles promptly rose to his feet and strode to the front. He lost no time in pleasantries.

'Chairman and Christian friends, this is not the first time the Eclectic Society has discussed this topic. Other societies, such as the London Missionary Society and

---

7. So strong that it could almost be felt or touched.
8. Acceptable way of proceeding.

the Baptist Missionary Society, have been formed. We, in the established Church of England, should not be lagging behind. I respect Mr Grant's knowledge and the reasoning behind the proposal, but I feel that the time has come for a more radical policy.

To help us, I propose three questions: What can we do? When shall we do it? How shall we do it?'

There was stirring in the gathering. Simeon's incisiveness[9] and urgency had gripped them.

'We need more than resolutions. We need something definite, something to stir people up. When? Immediately. Not a moment is to be lost. How? It is hopeless to wait for missionaries to be trained. Send out catechists[10] now!'

The meeting continued, thoroughly roused by Charles's speech. It ended with a decision to form a society and to meet again to flesh out the proposal. This meeting was held on 12th April, 1799 at the wonderfully named Castle and Falcon Inn in Aldersgate, London. It was chaired by the Rev John Venn. It formed 'The Mission to Africa and the East'. Its constitution was established. It had to be careful not to tread on toes because there were two existing missionary societies, the Society for Propagating Christian Knowledge and the Society for Propagating the Gospel. However, their activities were confined to British dominions, that is to countries ruled by Britain as part of its empire.

---

9. Getting to the point quickly

10. A teacher using a question and answer means of instruction

The society became known as the Church Missionary Society in 1812, and, despite a slow start, made a major contribution to mission and also evangelicalism in the Church of England. Charles was a major impetus behind the mission. With great enthusiasm, he flung himself into the society's work, going on deputation tours on the Society's behalf and speaking at most of their annual meetings for the next twenty years. He was enrolled as an Honorary Life Governor and honoured to preach the valedictory sermon to a group of missionaries about to sail overseas in 1817.

A Love for the Jews

Great though Charles's zeal for mission was, and important though his contribution to the founding of the Church Missionary Society was, his love for Jewish mission was equally intense and significant. He was pleased when the Archbishop of Canterbury gave his approval for the consecration of the Jewish Chapel at Bethnal Green in London. But it was not all plain sailing. By 1814 it was in debt, so he approached his friend, William Wilberforce, seeking help. He went to Barham Court in Kent instead of Wilberforce's London residence.

* * *

'William, how good of you to agree to see me here in Barham Court. No doubt you are glad to escape the pressure of Parliament for a pleasant break. How blessed we are to have people like you at the seat of parliamentary power,' said Charles to William Wilberforce.

'I don't know that my opponents in the House of Commons would necessarily agree. To them I am an anti-slavery bore, always yapping at their heels.'

'Yap on, William. The name of Wilberforce is now well known and final victory will be yours. But, as you know, there is another pressing matter I want to consult you on. I have a deep concern for bringing the gospel to the Jews. Well, it is a matter of grief to me that the London Jews' Society is not functioning as it should.'

William pursed his lips and frowned. 'What is the problem?'

'Well, for one thing, it is not well run. I would prefer it under church control. But more disastrously, it is in considerable debt.'

'How considerable, Charles?'

'Very considerable – £12,500[1]. A veritable mountain of debt.'

'How did that happen?'

'Well, partly it was due to mismanagement. Also having the Church of England and dissenters[2] working together didn't lend itself to smooth running. Finally, neither the church authorities nor the dissenters would pay for the Jewish chapel in Bethnal Green.'

'A sad tale indeed. So what do you propose to do?'

'Well, obviously this situation weighs heavily on me. But there is hope. There is one man, Lewis Way, who has unexpectedly come into a fortune and is prepared to give very generously. But first we need a plan to set the London Jews' Society – to give it its short name – on a

---

1. Worth over a million pounds today.
2. Those who would not join the Church of England but formed separate churches.

proper footing. I am struggling, I confess, to formulate a plan. I have with me four plans I have drawn up, yet none of them fully satisfies me. I am hoping that by applying yourself to this matter, you might come up with a plan which will satisfy me and convince Mr Way to help clear the debt.'

'Certainly, Charles. I am very happy to help. I would love to meet Mr Way, also. He seems very generous-hearted.'

'Indeed. Now, I know you are a busy man. Here are the four plans I drew up. Let me know what you think about them and how we should proceed. May God guide your thinking!'

'I will set my mind to it immediately.'

The plan rescued the London Society for Propagating Christianity Amongst the Jews (to give it its long title) and set it on a better footing. It became a Church of England sanctioned body, with better organisation and, between Mr Way and other supporters, the debt was paid off.

* * *

Charles rubbed his hands together. He was full of excitement and delight. For over two years the London Jews' Society had languished and had needed a boost. Now a deputation[3] of four men were about to embark on an exploratory trip through Europe, perhaps even as far as Jerusalem. These men included Lewis Way, whose money had helped clear the debt; Nehemiah Solomon,

---

3. A group of people appointed to undertake a mission.

a converted Jew from Poland who had been ordained a deacon in the Church of England; and Sultan Kategarry, a converted Muslim from Astrakhan in the far south of Russia. Now these men had been commissioned and were ready to set out.

'Gentlemen, what an encouraging service that was. My heart leaps with praise to God. But for you there may be many discouragements ahead,' said Charles.

'The God of Abraham, Isaac and Jacob will be with us. The Messiah will seek out his lost sheep,' intoned Nehemiah through his wiry, black beard.

'True, it is daunting, Charles,' commented Lewis, 'but it is also exciting. Just think – we have an invitation to meet the Emperor of Russia.'

'Yes, I was a Russian citizen, but Moscow is nearly 900 miles away and I would have no chance of seeing him as part of a crowd, far less speaking to him!' joined in Sultan Kategarry.

'You are right, of course,' said Charles. 'I was thrilled when the Emperor Alexander sent asking for Hebrew New Testaments and missionaries. The translation into Hebrew will shortly be completed. The chapel which I have purchased in Amsterdam is getting established and I hope to visit there. I believe God is calling us to make a special effort to bring his ancient people back to himself. What a blessing that would be to the world!'

'May we be used in some small way,' added Lewis.

'Well, I will be praying for you every day throughout your arduous journeyings,' promised Charles. 'I feel our parting like that of the parting of Paul and the Ephesian elders in Acts. I will soon be in tears.'

* * *

'Lewis, how good to see you again! Now, let me see, yes, it must be a full sixteen months since I saw you off to Russia.'

'Yes, Charles, in one way it seems like no time at all because we have packed in so much and been so busy, and yet it seems like ages ago in another way because we have been among so many different cultures and peoples.'

'Time is such a funny thing. A day may fly past and an hour may seem endless. Now tell me about your trip.'

'Well, Charles, I will tell more of my story when I report to the Jews' Society meeting, but I will tell you about some encouraging highlights.'

'You have my undivided attention.'

'The first major concentration of Jews we visited was in Warsaw. It has a huge ghetto[4]. Now many of the Jews there seems very open to the gospel and we had stimulating conversations. As a result, we thought it vital to seize the opportunity and left Nehemiah Solomon there. He has the tremendous advantage of knowing both Polish and Hebrew and seemed an ideal fit.'

'You acted wisely, I think. But the scriptural pattern I believe, is to go out two by two, so it would be good

---

4. A part of a city where Jews were forced to live in the past.

to send out another co-worker. I believe I know the very one – Friedenburgh, who is a converted Jew.'

'I have heard of him and trust your judgment regarding him. Nehemiah will be delighted.'

'What about the Russian capital, St Petersburg?'

'The welcome we received in St Petersburg was very courteous but also warm. It is a place of great magnificence with astonishingly grand and ornate palaces. These form a complete contrast to the miserable living conditions of the poor, including numerous Jews. But many Jews have also done very well and there is considerable resentment towards them because of that.'

'Yes, I hear that in parts of Germany and eastern Europe there lingers a deeply mistaken hatred of the Jews. But carry on.'

'Well, we visited synagogues and were treated with a mixture of kindness and suspicion, but we also met with converted Jews who begged us to help teach them. They were so grateful for the Scriptures.'

'What about the emperor?'

'That was astonishing. We thought that, perhaps after all, we might just see some minister for internal affairs, but not only were we introduced to the emperor and his entourage[5] in a splendid palace, but we had several meetings with him. As you know, he is favourably disposed towards missionaries and the spread of the Hebrew Scriptures among the two million

---

5. A group of people who work for and travel with a famous person while travelling.

Jews in Russia. He has also promised his protection to anyone who becomes a Christian. Any Jew who becomes a Christian will be given land to settle on. The door is wide open.'

'Wonderful, though we must be careful not to offer worldly inducements[6] to conversion. It must be a true heart renewal, a work of the Spirit of God.'

'But there is even more. I was invited to an international congress at Aix-la-Chapelle. There were important dignitaries[7] from five leading countries including our Foreign Minister, Viscount Castlereagh, and Metternich, the Austrian Minister for Foreign Affairs. I was invited to submit a proposal outlining how to advance the prosperity of the Jews and the work of the gospel among them. It was duly accepted by the congress and signed. I was and am amazed.'

'The Lord does wondrous things which we look not for. My prayers have been graciously heard. You have really whetted my appetite for your report to the Jews' Society. And talking of whetting appetites, I have roast partridges just waiting to be eaten! Come and dine.'

* * *

There were only two occasions on which Charles Simeon left British soil, and both were in connection with Jewish mission. The first was in 1818 when

---

6. Things which entice or persuade.

7. People of importance or high office.

he went along with his friend, Rev William Marsh, minister at Colchester, to Holland to familiarise himself with the work of the gospel among Jewish people, especially in Amsterdam, where there were at least 25,000 Jews.

* * *

'Well, William, we are about to set off again for our home territory. Do you think our trip was worthwhile?'

'Most certainly, Charles. It is tremendously encouraging that the Dutch seem to have enlightened views towards the Jews. The edict of the King of Holland, requiring that Jews be educated in the Hebrew Scriptures in their own tongue, was a remarkable one and by your efforts you have made the lackadaisical[8] Dutch authorities take action to see it become a reality.'

'Yes, that pleased me. I also enjoyed talking to the Jewish physician, Dr Cappadose. He was very open but sceptical of the motives of his relations who have accepted Christianity. Because the Jews are treated equally here and feel comfortable, he thought that we would not make any impact, but I assured him that the help we were bringing was spiritual, not worldly. I am sure there will be many other intelligent people like him who are open-minded, but it is not the work of one afternoon to deal effectively with them.'

---

8. Showing no enthusiasm.

'I think being here at the day commemorating the victory at Waterloo[9] was also good. It showed the common ground we have with the Dutch.'

'True, William. There is abundant scope here for the right workers, I think. We must pray the Lord of the harvest that labourers, who are fit to be sent out, will offer themselves. I am pleased that we now have a chapel here in Amsterdam as a base for our work.'

* * *

The next trip was to Paris, five years later, in 1823. Lewis Way ministered in a chapel there and Charles preached to an audience of 500. He was very pleased with progress there. However, Paris did not seem to appeal to him as he wrote in his diary for Monday, 11th April: *Left Paris, to my great joy.*

His zeal for the work of the gospel among the Jews did not abate with age. Even in the last six or seven years of his life, he often made the journey to London to the Jews' Society committee meetings, leaving very early in the morning.

He never set his zeal for mission among Jews against his enthusiasm for mission to the Gentiles[10]. Charles never felt that Gentile mission lost out through Jewish mission. Based on Romans chapter 11, he believed that the Scriptures teach that great blessing will come to

---

9. The Battle of Waterloo was fought in 1815. It was the final defeat for the French Emperor Napoleon. He had conquered large parts of Europe, so his downfall was celebrated.
10. A Jewish term for non-Jews.

the world, through the Jews, near the end times. Not everyone felt that way about Jewish mission. At one meeting he was sitting on the platform next to Edward Bickersmith of the Church Missionary Society. Jealous on behalf of his own society's work, Bickersmith wrote on a piece of paper which he handed to Charles, 'Six million Jews and six hundred million Gentiles – which is most important?' The reply was not long in coming: 'But if the conversion of the six is to be the life from the dead to the six hundred million, what then?' He held two things in balance: the deep and continuing love of God for his ancient people; and his extraordinary grace in including Gentiles as members of his people.

On the last occasion he delivered a sermon to the annual meeting, he referred to the use Paul makes of the image of the olive tree branches in Romans chapter 11. Paul pictures the Jewish people as an olive tree. Paul thinks of the Jews who rejected Jesus as branches cut out of the good olive tree. 'God helping me', said Charles Simeon, 'I will never cease to labour till I have been the happy means of re-installing one withered branch into its own olive-tree. For this I will labour; for this I will pray. For this I will combine my exertions with others.'

On his deathbed he even composed an address on the subject of the Jews to be read out to undergraduates. He was a true gospel friend to Jews.

Charles Simeon and the Church of England

Charles Simeon was not exclusive. He greatly supported the work of the British and Foreign Bible Society, which was comprised of Christians of different groupings. He greatly admired and was in correspondence with Thomas Chalmers, an outstanding Scottish minister in the first half of the nineteenth century. One of his great friends, Joseph Gurney, was a Quaker. He had a warm relationship with William Jay, the popular congregational minister in Bath. He read to his students the accounts of missionary work in the journal of the Baptist Missionary Society. But he was always loyal to the Church of England and very comfortable with its form of worship. He worshipped in the Presbyterian manner on his trips to Scotland but was always glad to get back to the Church of England form of church service.

His love for the Church of England was, despite its lack of love for him when he was ordained, not because it valued him. He was a lonely figure, initially, until he established and built up a network of friends. He was opposed by bishops. For example, one objected to him starting a Bible Society in Cambridge. Even students who were seen as his followers suffered. One was denied an academic prize he fully deserved on the basis of his 'Simeonism'. Evangelicals recognised the authority of the Bible, preached Christ crucified as the only way to acceptance with God and insisted on the absolute need for new birth by the Holy Spirit. They were, if not despised, shunned as brain-fevered fanatics. It was one of Charles's achievements – along with his friends and followers – to make evangelicals a respected and influential group within the Church of England.

How did he do this? One way was to be very polite to those in authority and recognise their position. He was deferential[1], never rude. Here is a part of a letter he wrote to William Wilberforce discussing young curates: *The truth is, that young men act very imprudently, and in a very bad spirit, and compel the bishop to proceed against them; and then call it persecution ...'*

He was also wise. He wished zeal to be mixed with wisdom. Here is a parable he used in a letter to a hot-headed young man seeking a curacy.

Two ships were aground at London Bridge. The proprietors of one sent for a hundred horses; and pulled it to pieces. The proprietor of the other waited for the tide; and with sails and rudders directed it as they pleased.

The lesson is obvious! Patience and self-control are included in the fruit of the Spirit.

---

1. Respectful.

What was the result of this patience? In later years he was consulted on matters by bishops. On one occasion he was visited by three bishops – the Bishop of Bath and Wells, the Bishop of Salisbury and the Bishop of Limerick in Ireland. For an hour he showed them round King's College and Trinity Library. Afterwards, he commented: *In former years I should as soon have expected a visit from three crowned heads, as from three persons wearing a mitre*[2] *... because my religious character affixed a stigma to my name.*

But it wasn't just his character which won over the suspicious and the downright hostile and caused evangelicals to have a greater impact. He was practical and an organiser.

* * *

Charles paid the cab driver and waited for a moment or two while the clatter of the horse's hooves receded. Then he strode up to the imposing front door of Wilberforce's house in Kensington and pulled the doorbell.

He was ushered into the reception room and sat down. A moment later, William entered and grasped him by the hand.

'Charles, how good to see you. What brings you to this wicked city?'

'I have come for a meeting of the Jews' Society, but I have a couple of hours to spare. I had heard that you were not well.'

---

2. A bishop's hat.

'Yes, I had ten days in bed, but I'm somewhat better. My eyesight is getting poor, too. But enough of complaints! I am feeling much better for seeing you. Believing fellowship is such a tonic. It cheers soul and strengthens the body – mine at least!'

'Well, I am sure I will go away refreshed, too. Tell me, how are things in parliament?'

'Well, as you know, we won a great victory in stopping the slave trade, but we are pressing on to try to have slavery itself abolished in the dominions. But my name is continually blackened and vicious things are said, which are not fit to be repeated. But what about you? How is Cambridge?'

'There were some difficulties with those who were given some responsibility and developed a lordly attitude, but they left and all is peace. I am very pleased at the way curates, and others who attend my conversation classes, have turned out. I try to teach them to preach.'

'But isn't that a burden on you? You have services and visits and correspondence and work with societies and university responsibilities – and not even a wife to help you. Have you thought of marrying?'

'I have, William, I have. But I do feel that Cambridge is my calling. Being a spiritual father and tutor to future curates and vicars – and bishops, too, who knows? –gives me great joy. So many Cambridge graduates go on to serve in the church and it would be a great means of transforming the evangelical character of the church if they are solidly grounded and equipped for ministry.'

'Hmm, I see. You know that I can procure a well-paid place of ministry for you, where you would be vicar? But I can see from your grand plan that any pleading on my part would be futile.'

'I am convinced that I am in the right place. I look back on some of those I have nurtured – Henry Martyn, Thomas Thomason, John Sargent – and cannot but believe that Cambridge is where God has placed me.'

'I would not dissuade you.'

'I have another reason for calling on you, perhaps related to what I have discussed with you about spreading the evangelical witness of our church.'

'Go ahead, Charles.'

'Well, you know how John Thornton, Henry's father, bought the right to propose ministers[3] to the church authorities when the former minister died, retired or moved to another church?'

'I have heard about it, but I don't know too much about it. Henry is my cousin, of course, and John was a wonderful man of faith.'

'Indeed, William. And I greatly admire Henry, too. Well, my idea is to build on John's idea. I want to form a Trust[4] which will buy the right to propose who should fill vacant ministries to parishes throughout the land. Evangelicals will run the Trust and ensure that the

---

3. The bishop had the final say but usually accepted the proposed person.
4. A legally recognised organisation that invests money for a purpose.

present difficulties which evangelicals have in becoming vicars and rectors will be eased. By setting up the Trust, we will ensure that the right of proposing who should be the next minister will continue into the foreseeable future. What do you think? I value your opinion.'

'I think you have taken a good idea and made it a brilliant one. The Lord bless you in your plan and revive our church. Now, the time is passing and we have been talking a while. Let us pray for what we have been discussing.'

'A splendid suggestion, William.'

* * *

To this very day, the trust still operates in England and the United States. Simeon's influence was immense in the first half of the nineteenth century church. It is estimated that by the end of his life, one third of Church of England ministers had sat under his preaching. The nineteenth century historian and writer, Lord Macaulay, said of him: *As to Simeon, if you knew what his authority and influence were, and how they extended from Cambridge to the most remote corners of England, you would allow that his real sway over the Church was far greater than that of any Primate[5].* His godliness was one reason for this, but another was his vision and practical good sense.

---

5. Archbishop.

His Wider Influence

Charles' influence with university undergraduates, bishops, the Eclectic Society, chaplains sent to India, the Church Missionary Society, Jewish mission and the evangelical movement is clear. Nearly all of it, however, is within the confines of the Church of England. So did his ministry spread wider than the national church?

The answer is yes. Though he found weaknesses in the inter-denominational organisations like the London Missionary Society, which prompted the formation of the Church Missionary Society, he was a very enthusiastic supporter of the British and Foreign Bible Society. The origin of the society was in Wales. The story is often told of the Welsh-speaking Mary Jones who walked twenty miles to Bala to obtain a Welsh Bible. The Bala minister, Rev Thomas Charles, was determined to help the people of Wales read the Bible in their own language. A Baptist minister, Rev Joseph Hughes, demanded of other church leaders on 7th December 1802, 'Surely a society might be formed for the purpose; and if for Wales, why not for the kingdom? If for the kingdom, why not for the world?' At the London Tavern, in Bishopsgate in the capital, on 7th March, around three hundred, including William Wilberforce, met and formed the British and Foreign Bible Society. It was broadly evangelical in scope with no denominational barriers. Its committee included friends of Charles Simeon, such as Charles Grant, Zachary Macaulay, Granville Sharp, James Stephen and others of the Clapham Sect.

In 1811, an auxiliary branch of the British and Foreign Bible Society was formed in Cambridge at the request of students. The inaugural meeting had among the speakers the local MP, two professors and Dr Isaac Milner of Queens' College. The Bishop of Peterborough opposed its formation, however. It was also opposed by Dr Marsh, Professor of Divinity at Cambridge, basically because it was not solely Church of England. Never daunted by opposition, Charles Simeon publicly opposed him. So also did Isaac Milner. Charles thought that Isaac Milner had done an excellent job in demolishing Dr Marsh's arguments. Others joined in and Dr Marsh admitted that he would be as well trying to stem the flow of lava from a volcano! Through other controversies, too, Charles was a loyal supporter of the society.

But if his support for the British and Foreign Bible Society shows that he used his influence in wider spheres, this is made far clearer in his visits to Scotland. The first visit was in May 1796, after he had established friendly relationships with the Rev Dr Walter Buchanan, minister of the Canongate Church in Edinburgh.

'Dear Walter, how blessed I am to meet you on your home territory,' enthused Charles, grasping Walter's hand firmly. 'I feel so drawn to you as a brother in Christ.'

'It is my privilege to welcome you to Edinburgh. I so look forward to spending time with you and having soul fellowship in the Lord.'

'Yes, Walter, I look forward to special times together and am sure that our bond in the Lord will grow. I am so impressed with the castle and the magnificent views over the Firth of Forth, but these pleasures do not compare with our Lord's glory.'

'Now, Charles, while you are here, I want you to hear some of our prominent preachers – but I also wish you to preach, because I am sure that you will be well-received.'

'Well, Walter, you are an optimistic fellow. A prayer book man from a church with bishops and an Englishman, too. What would John Knox have said?' asked Charles, teasingly.

'Times have changed. Nor should you forget that John Knox ministered in England and his supporters only managed to deliver us from the stranglehold of the French with English help! No one will be throwing stools at you like Jenny Geddes did![1]'

'As you say, times have changed. I am reassured.'

'Now, I have asked a young man to come along in an hour's time. His name is James Haldane. He is from a wealthy background. He is a man of leisure but also a man with a heart burning with zeal for the spread of the gospel. Now, when you are in Scotland it would be good for you to see something of the Highlands, so he has kindly volunteered to escort you. You love horses, so he will arrange a good horse for you. I am sure that you will enjoy his companionship.'

'You are truly thoughtful. I could not wish for a better organiser.'

* * *

Charles enjoyed his time in Edinburgh. He loved how Walter preached Scripture and he thought the zeal of the grand old man of the evangelical party in the Church of Scotland, Dr Erskine, reminded him of his own mentor, Henry Venn of Yelling, but he did not enjoy the length of a four and a half hour communion service! While in Scotland, he adapted to the way Scottish people worshipped. His Church of England conscience was not disturbed because the monarch, though head of the Church of England, worships in the national church in Scotland, so, as Charles put it, 'Where a king *must*

---

1. When the English form of prayer book prescribed service was introduced – on the orders of the Archbishop of Canterbury – in St Giles Church in Edinburgh in 1637, Jenny Geddes objected and threw a stool at the minister reading the prayer book. A disturbance followed.

attend, a clergyman *may* preach.' He made his mark as a preacher and, once his reputation was established, he was heard by 3,000 people on one occasion.

During his first visit to Scotland, he went to Lady Ross' grounds. Here he saw blind men weaving. They had just been taught a little in the asylum[2] at Edinburgh. One of the blind men, aged twenty-eight, on being questioned about his knowledge of spiritual things, answered, 'I never saw till I was blind; nor did I ever know contentment when I had my eyesight as I do now that I have lost it. I can truly affirm, though few know how to credit me, that I would on no account change my present situation and circumstances with any that I ever enjoyed before I was blind.' He had only become blind at the age of twenty-five, but since then had had his spiritual eyes opened to the beauty of Jesus Christ the Saviour.

However, even that memorable conversation was not the highlight of his visit. That came later when he was touring the Highlands with James Haldane.

He enjoyed praying with James on mountain tops and distributing gospel tracts. One Communion Sunday in Moulin, a village outside Pitlochry in Gaelic-speaking Perthshire, there was a Communion service where believers took bread and wine in remembrance of Christ's sacrifice on the cross. Only so many could sit at the table at one time and as there were 1,000 or more people there to take part, there were several groups of

---

2. A place where people at risk are cared for.

people who would come forward to take Communion, and each group was given a short address. Charles gave two addresses and then preached again in the evening.

'James, I am glad to be back at the manse here in Moulin. I felt lethargic today when I preached, but the small number who understood English seemed attentive enough.'

'Yes, I feel that there is a lack of zeal and power and life here. There is a need for the outpouring of the Spirit.'

'Yes, I warned against formality in religion, but only the Spirit can give life in our souls.'

'I think Mr Stewart is just arriving. No doubt we will have a fine meal to revive us.'

* * *

Later, the local minister, Alexander Stewart, and Charles Simeon had a private conversation.

'Come in, come in, Dr Stewart. You have provided a fine, comfortable room for me and I am grateful for your hospitality. The meal was excellent.'

'Well, Mr Simeon, the Highland people have always been known for their hospitality, even in the lawless times in previous ages.'

'Now, I think you have something on your mind when you wish to converse with me alone.'

'Well, Mr Simeon, I felt some stirring of my soul when you said a few words after our dinner. But I do feel that my ministry is unprofitable. I am not satisfied in my own soul with my spiritual state. I feel that I am upright but cold.'

'I appreciate your honesty. Not everyone is prepared to bare his soul even to a fellow minister. There are two key things I would say to you. Reflect on the cross. Reflect on the dying love of Christ. Reflect on the breadth and the length and the depth and the height of the love of Christ. These things will kindle love to God and love to God will kindle zeal in your ministry.'

'I see. Perhaps I have been urging duty and thinking of the teaching rather than the sacrifice of Jesus.'

'Yes – and remember it was so personal for Paul. He wrote of the Christ who 'loved me and gave himself for me.' Do you think of Jesus in that way?'

Dr Stewart was silent. Then there was a catch in his voice as he asked, 'What is the second point?'

'You must plead with God to liven your soul by his Holy Spirit. You need the life of God in your soul. You then need the anointing of the Spirit on your ministry.'

Again there was a choked silence. Then Dr Stewart asked, 'Can you pray for me?'

'Tender and gracious God, Father to all who truly trust in you, show us your redeeming love in Christ. May the body broken for us and the blood shed for us stir up our souls and affections. Bless Dr Stewart with a sense of forgiveness and joy in the Lord. Encourage and make him fruitful in the work of the gospel. In Jesus' precious name, Amen.'

'Truly, Mr Simeon, the Lord sent you to Moulin. You have been a true spiritual friend to me.'

* * *

After that visit, Dr Stewart's ministry was transformed. There was a correspondence between them in which Simeon prayed, 'that what you now experience may only be as the drop before the shower.' The prayer was indeed answered. Dr Stewart wrote to Charles to tell him of a poor, frail old lady who had been blessed by Charles's preaching. Wonderfully, through the prayer meetings held in that woman's hovel and through the new evangelical note in Alexander Stewart's preaching, three years later a wonderful revival spread through Moulin and many were truly converted.

Charles visited Scotland again in 1798 and travelled as far north as Tain. But because the excesses of the French revolution had alarmed conservative people and, amazingly enough, evangelicals were suspected of being in sympathy with the revolutionaries, the General Assembly in 1799 banned people who were not ordained in Scotland from preaching in Scottish pulpits. Later, this was relaxed. Charles visited Scotland in 1815 and again for the last time in 1819. One reason for his later visits was to raise money for Jewish mission. In 1819, he raised 500 guineas for the Jews and Bible societies. Anti-semitism was never a problem in Scotland and the huge amount of money donated to the Jews' Society as a result of his visits show that there was popular support for the Jews some time before the famous mission of discovery to Palestine by Robert Murray McCheyne, Andrew Bonar and others in 1839. Simeon had a very fruitful and blessed connection with Scotland.

Preacher and Spiritual Guide

So why did Charles Simeon make such an impact? He had considerable drawbacks – he was too much of a sharp dresser, he could fly off the handle, he was self-important, his congregation was against him, he was cold-shouldered by other academics and any who drank in his teaching were mocked and labelled 'Sims'. We could answer that it was the Lord's will to make him a means of blessing to others. That would be perfectly true. We could give various answers based on his devotional practices and his developing character, but absolutely central to his impact and ministry was the study and preaching of the Scriptures. He was first and foremost a preacher.

So what kind of preacher was he? Right back in chapter three we saw that his first preaching for Mr Atkinson stirred up much interest locally. But, looking back, Charles would not have placed much store by it. A friend said it was 'crude and undigested'. Indeed, his own verdict on his early preaching was far from complimentary: *When I first began to write I knew no more than a brute how to make a sermon.*

This of course changed. He read a book which influenced him and which enabled him to develop a style of preaching in which faithfulness to Scripture, clarity and focus were combined with immense earnestness. Because of that he believed that those called to be preachers could be taught how to preach and he started preaching classes with students wishing to become heralds of the gospel. He preached from notes, never a written out sermon. He had wise but definite views about sermons. Here is a specimen of his wisdom and memorable, vivid style: *A sermon should be like a telescope: each successive division of it should be as an additional lens to bring the subject of your text nearer and make it more distinct.*

* * *

'Mr Simeon, what do you consider the most serious fault in the way we preach the gospel?'

'Now, that is a question, Thomas. We might mention mumbling and feebleness of voice, because what is the use of a preacher whom they cannot hear? We might mention hesitancy because the gospel is so glorious that it is to be declared confidently as the best of all possible tidings. But I think that worse than these is a dull, mechanical performance of a duty. I cannot abide that matter-of-form spirit which makes the solemnities of God's house and of worship, a mere business without reality.'

'But what about set prayers? And what about homilies – which are just written sermons, are they not? How can we stop being mechanical?'

'It is a problem, John. In Scotland they have no set prayers. But prayers without a form can be rambling and lack reverence. If all men could pray at all times as some men pray some of the time, I would welcome praying freely. But the set prayers are beautiful and carefully thought out. What we need to do is to prepare our hearts and to meditate on the prayers so that they become our prayers from the heart, not just a read order of service. That is how to stop becoming mechanical.'

'No one would accuse you of heartless, cold preaching, Mr Simeon. Is that the reason people are starting to flock to Trinity Church?'

'Forcefulness must be combined with the truth and with reliance on God. But salvation is not a trifling matter. Mr Brown told me of a little girl in church who whispered to her mother, 'O Mama, what is the gentleman in a passion about?' Okay, we can smile at the little girl, but I would prefer to be passionate than lifeless. I preach wholeheartedly to the people with my tongue, my eyes and my hands. The great aim of preaching, as you know, is firstly, to humble the sinner; secondly to exalt the Saviour; thirdly, to promote holiness. They are all of them tremendous tasks.'

* * *

Imagine then, what it would have been like for Charles when in 1807, after twenty-five years of ministry, he took ill and his voice – which he said 'should be as music' – gave way. As we have seen, Simeon had curates who helped out, and his voice gradually improved enough for him to resume limited preaching, but sometimes with an enfeebled voice. For a man of energy and preaching zeal, this was a trial.

He himself attributed that to a lesson from God. He had reckoned on working at full capacity until he was sixty and then relaxing his efforts. However, God had other ideas. It was not till Charles was sixty and crossing the border into Scotland for his last trip there, that all of a sudden he felt 'perceptibly revived'. From that moment on, he was full of renewed vigour. There was no more thought of retirement! He would die in harness like Moses!

* * *

Because he wished to be a teacher and leave a legacy, Charles undertook the massive task of combining all his sermons into a mammoth preacher's commentary on the Bible. It covered twenty-one volumes, none of them slim! It was a huge task for the printers, too, because Charles was very pernickety and scrutinised the proofs for every tiny mistake. When it was completed, he was delighted and copies were sent to various important people such as the King of Great Britain and Ireland and the Archbishop of Canterbury.

The explanations of passages of Scripture were sermon notes and expanded comments on the passage. Charles was at pains to let Scripture speak for itself. He did not like it when preachers made Scripture fit their thoughts. Instead, our thoughts should be moulded by

Scripture. Discover and then decide what the passage says, is the kind of advice he gave to preachers.

* * *

Gifted and arresting preacher though he was, his teaching ministry was not limited to his pulpit, nor was it limited to his conversation classes or preaching classes. One way he had of teaching and giving wise advice was through correspondence. If he was alive today, he would be busy with his e-mails. He was very thorough and painstaking in organising his letters – all 7,000 of them! He kept copies of all the letters he sent. This was very helpful for biographers.

Many of his letters were sent to people seeking advice. One common problem people experience is that they feel low because they cannot find peace with God. He wrote wise words to somebody wrestling with this problem:

You are too much occupied in looking at yourself and too little in beholding the Lord Jesus Christ. It is ... by [this] that you are to be changed into the divine image. You want a greater measure of holiness to warrant [give good ground for] your confidence in the divine promises; when it is only by apprehending [grasping] those promises that you can attain the holiness you are seeking after.

In other words, the person is looking to personal holiness for assurance that Christ is his or her Saviour, rather than to Christ, the source of holiness and assurance. The person has the cart before the horse.

To another person complaining of prayers going no higher than the ceiling, he wrote: *The sigh, the groan of a broken heart, will soon go through the ceiling up to heaven, aye, into the very bosom of God.*

But it was not just by preached or taught or written words that he commended the Saviour. His Quaker friend, John Gurney, said of him: *His faithful love and affection, and his warm bright cheering views of religion, have often been a source of comfort to me in times of trouble and sorrow.* In other words, he lived in such a way as to commend the Saviour and teach by example.

Final Days

John Wesley once said, 'Our people die well.' That could certainly be said of Charles Simeon.

Charles was ordinarily of good health, but he, as we have seen, did lose his voice at one point. Also, he had severe attacks of the crippling illness gout. Gout causes severe pains in the joints, particularly the feet. It must have been one of these attacks in 1834 that meant his death was mis-reported in Cambridge. He might have said with the American writer Mark Twain, 'The reports of my death have been greatly exaggerated!' In 1835, he wrote to a friend, telling him that he was 'preaching at seventy-six with all the exuberance of youth'.

In 1836, too, he was feeling strong and vigorous. In August of that year he said, 'Yesterday I preached to a church as full as it could hold.' He was asked to preach the university sermon in November, an invitation which he accepted. Yet he knew that his life here could be of short duration and he had longings for heaven. In a letter to a friend in July he wrote: *I am almost counting the hours till I reach my sweet abode*. His last sermon was preached on Sunday, 18th September. In that sermon, he said, 'Whatever your attainments may be, and whatever you may have done or suffered in the service of your God, you must forget the things that are behind, till you have actually fulfilled your course and obtained the crown.'

On Wednesday, 21st September, 1836 he went over to Ely to pay his respects to the new bishop, Dr Allen. However, it was not the best of days – damp and chilly. Charles did not take the precaution of a topcoat. The bishop was very pleasant to him and suggested a tour of the cathedral together. They lingered too long on the tour. The vast space of the splendid cathedral was unheated. By the time he had travelled back to Cambridge through the raw, grey weather over the fenland, a chill had set in. There were moments of rallying, and one day he ventured out, but he never truly recovered.

He realised that this would be his last illness. He was fully reconciled to this and accepted it as the will of God. Friends, including his curate William Carus (Charles never referred to his curates as 'my curate' but always as 'my brother') were impressed by how patient Charles was throughout this period of suffering.

* * *

'Mr Carus, I am amazed at how patient and tranquil Mr Simeon is,' commented Dr Haviland.

'You are right, Doctor. He often used to complain of his old weakness of temper, but there are no traces of it now.'

'He seems so in possession of his mental abilities. I really thought he was about to go when we gathered round him a couple of days ago. He was very clear that he did not want what he called a dying scene.'

'I remember his exact words. "That I abhor from my inmost soul. I wish to be alone, with my God, the lowest of the low." He is very patient, but he still has that characteristic firmness of view.'

'Don't you think that he took too severe a view of himself? I mean – "the lowest of the low"?'

'Well, Doctor, he himself would tell you, if he were not so ill, that it is in the brightness of the light that blots and blemishes are discovered. He would say that the nearer to God he is, the more he needs to humble himself for his sins and failures. As the Scriptures say, "God is light and in him there is no darkness."'

'I am sure Mr Simeon could not have put it better, Mr Carus. I will be back tomorrow to see how our patient is doing. In the meantime, the nurse will keep an eye on him.'

* * *

During moments when the illness receded he was not inactive, working out sermons and a talk about the Jewish mission. One thing which especially gladdened his heart was that, on 3rd November, he received a letter from the Bishop of Ely telling him that Mr Carus, his beloved curate, had been appointed as his successor. Mr Carus had been entrusted with his documents and letters and would go on to write his memoirs.

From then on, he became very weak and spent his time meditating on passages of Scripture. For example, he spent hours reflecting on the last verse of Romans chapter 11 and repeating to himself the words, 'For of him, and through him, and to him, are all things: to whom be glory for ever.'

One attending him in his illness recorded the following: 'He said, "Soon I will behold all the glorified saints and angels around the throne of my God and Saviour, who has loved me unto death, and given himself for me; then I shall see him whom having not seen I love; in whom, though now I see him not, yet believing I rejoice with joy unspeakable and full of glory." Turning his eyes towards me, he added, "Of the reality of this I am as sure as if I were there this moment."'

On Sunday, 13th November, at ten minutes after two o'clock, when the bell of St Mary's, not far off, had just ceased to call the congregation to the University sermon, he breathed his last and then rested with his Lord.

Simeon's will was opened, and was found to contain instructions regarding his desired place of burial: 'If I die out of College, I am not careful where my body shall be buried. But if I die in Cambridge, I should wish to be buried in my College Chapel.'

Accordingly, preparations were made to lay him in the great **vault** beneath the pavement in the outer chapel. Obviously, he did not think the place of burial of vast importance, but he had been in Cambridge University all his adult life and it was fitting for him to be buried at King's College.

Simeon had wished his funeral to be kept simple. Many of his ministerial friends had expressed a strong wish to be present, and consequently were invited; and the Provost gave private admission into the outer chapel to the congregation of Trinity Church; but apart from this no outside attendance was officially sanctioned. This was not to be a private occasion, however. All of the university wished to pay their respects to someone who was once cold-shouldered by the academic staff; and the flood-tide could not be held back. Heads of Houses, Doctors, Professors, Fellows, men of all ages, positions and views, and from every college, came to the burial of Charles Simeon. It was reckoned that there were about 1,500 from the university there alone.

It was Saturday, 19th November when the funeral took place. The town was busy with the usual market; but all the shops in the main streets were shut out of respect, and the iron railings east and north of the College were swarming with packed crowds of people. Almost no lectures or classes were held that day in the university, to allow heartfelt mourners to attend the funeral and to see his resting place.

The service itself was solemn and impressive and many of the congregation, young and old, were in tears. Charles Simeon had instructed his friend, Rev Dr William Dealtry, whom at one point he had helped to become successor to Rev John Venn at Clapham, that there was not to be a word of praise of him. All the glory was to go to God. There was a solemn procession with the coffin led by university dignitaries before it was laid in the vault. Nearly every bell of the university tolled to mark his passing.

In his church, a memorial was soon afterwards erected by the congregation. Appropriately, it was placed in the eastern part of the church beside memorials commemorating the life and labours of his former curates and dear friends Henry Martyn and Thomas Thomason. The decorative stone contains the following inscription:

THE REV. CHARLES SIMEON, M.A.,
Senior Fellow of King's College,
And fifty-four years vicar of this parish; who,
whether as the ground of his own hopes,
or as the subject of all his ministrations,
determined to know nothing but
JESUS CHRIST AND HIM CRUCIFIED.

The wording was based on what he himself had suggested. He obviously, and in keeping with his Christian character, wished to give Christ the glory.

That is how he wished his life summed up. Would it not be wonderful if we all could have that focus? You don't have to be a minister to put Christ first!

Charles Simeon
Timeline

World or political events of the times are in italics.

1759 Born in Reading, Berkshire, on 24th September.

1766 Entered Eton College.

1779 Went to Cambridge as an undergraduate and was converted.

1782 Became a Fellow of King's College, Cambridge, on 29th January, and ordained a deacon on 22nd May. He began preaching as volunteer locum (i.e. on a placement) at St Edward's.

His brother, William, died.

1783 Graduated B.A. in September and became curate-in-charge of Holy Trinity Church, Cambridge.

The Treaty of Paris was signed, ending the American War of Independence. Britain recognised the independence of its former American colonies, which became the United States of America.

1784 Charles Simeon's father died.

1789 *The Paris prison and fortress, the Bastille, was stormed by a mob on 14th July, one of the first acts of the French Revolution.*

1790 Started sermon-technique classes.

1796 First trip to Scotland.

1799 Formation of the Church Missionary Society.

1805 *Admiral Nelson won the naval battle of Trafalgar against the French on 21st October but died of his wounds.*

British naval power frustrated the ambitions of the French emperor Napoleon.

Henry Martyn sailed to India.

1807 Simeon lost his preaching voice.

The slave trade was abolished — but not slavery itself.

1808 Thomas Thomason sailed to India.

1812 Henry Martyn died in Turkey.

1813 The Simeon Trust started in order to fund more evangelical preachers in the Church of England.

1814 First Bishop of Calcutta appointed.

1815 *The Duke of Wellington won the Battle of Waterloo, defeating Napoleon.*

Trip to Scotland.

1819 *The Massacre of Peterloo in Manchester on 16th August. At least eighteen died after militia attacked a huge peaceful demonstration.*

Last trip to Scotland. Suddenly, at the age of sixty, Simeon's preaching voice came back!

1832 Parliament passed the Reform Act to reform the system of election of MPs, a major step to all adults having the right to vote in elections.

1833 Slavery Abolition Act abolished slavery in the British Empire.

William Wilberforce died.

1836 Simeon died and was buried in King's College Chapel.

Thinking Further Topics

Chapter 1: Early Years

Bible References: Psalm 78:5-6; Proverbs 2:1-5; Acts 22:3.

What is school like for you? No doubt it was very different from the experience of Charles Simeon. But all of us know about trying to impress people and be accepted. Despite the efforts of teachers nowadays to make learning interesting, there is always the need to put in the effort to absorb and retain skills and information.

In the Old Testament, parents were responsible for teaching their children God's law. We can see this in the reference to Proverbs, where King Solomon gives wise advice to his son. In the New Testament, schooling was often instruction of a small group of students by a learned person. This was the case with the Apostle Paul, who sat at the feet of the Jewish scholar Gamaliel.

Is school drudgery for you or do you see it as a privilege God has given? Have you thought about how millions are held back and live in poverty and suffering because they don't have the opportunity to go to school?

Chapter 2: Cambridge and Conversion

Bible Reference: Leviticus 16:21.

Why do people disregard Jesus and have no thought of church or salvation or eternity? One reason is that they feel no need. They have no sense of sin or guilt or of their conscience being troubled. Despite growing up unconcerned, Charles had enough sense to know that he was totally unfit to take Communion. Sometimes God uses experiences to make us realise just how unfit we are to be accepted by him and go to heaven. Have you ever felt like that?

If we realise that sin has made us unclean, what can we do? Often our instinct is to make up for our sins by trying to sort out our lives. That never works, because past sins need to be accounted for and, anyway, we can never live up to God's standards. Only God can remove our sin. He does that by providing a substitute. Jesus, by dying, paid the penalty of our sin. The innocent one died for, and in place of, the guilty. This is the great truth which brought relief and joy to Charles. How does Leviticus 16:21 provide a helpful picture of what Jesus has done for us?

Chapter 3: Becoming a Preacher
Bible reference: Luke 10:1-3.
Do your plans always go smoothly? Charles's plans certainly didn't. Despite his zeal – or maybe partly because of it – he faced determined opposition. This is the common experience of Christians. If you are open about going to church, or believing the Bible or even accepting that God created us male and female, not only friendships but also career prospects may suffer.

How can we face up to that? Well, God promises help. This help is known as grace because God is being kind to us. He never leaves us on our own, abandoned to hostility. He is always with us. We may be lambs in the middle of wolves, but we are still God's lambs.

We also need to think of Jesus and all he suffered. If he was prepared to suffer to a degree beyond our imagining on our behalf, should we not be prepared to suffer for him, even consider it a privilege? This is what Charles came to realise when he thought about Simon from Cyrene carrying Jesus' cross.

Chapter 4: Becoming Accepted

Bible references: Hebrews 6:12; Isaiah 55:10-11.

How do you deal with discouragement? Isn't it easy to give up – or at very least to lose the joy of the Lord?

Charles' remedy – and it comes straight from the Bible as the Scripture reference in Hebrews shows – was to exercise faith and patience.

Faith looks to the Lord and to his promises. One promise might be the one in Isaiah chapter 55. We have to trust that God will fulfil his promise to bless his Word.

Patience recognises that God is wise. His timing does not run according to our clocks. God's will trumps our will. Service is not about our frantic efforts or timetables but submission to our Saviour King.

Patience arises from faith. The next time we blurt out something rash or are discontented with slow progress, let us ask for faith and patience from the

God who loves to give generously without finding fault.

Chapter 5: Charles Simeon the Man

Bible references: Psalm 32:5; 1 John 1:8-9.

Do you ever confess your sins to God? Charles certainly did. He said that he 'loved the valley of humiliation.' This meant that he felt greatly blessed when he humbled himself before God and confessed his sins.

Refusing to acknowledge our sins is foolish and harmful. It is foolish because God sees all that goes on in our hearts as well as our actions, so to hide our sins is futile. It is harmful because it cuts us off from the remedy for our sins – which is the sacrifice for sin made by Jesus when he died on the cross. If we refuse to admit that we have sinned, we are not going to seek to have it dealt with by the sacrifice Jesus made.

Are you covering up sin?

Chapter 6: His Band of Brothers

Bible references Psalm 133:1; Philemon 15-16.

Have you good Christian friends? Is there a bond between you and others which comes from a shared trust in Jesus?

Paul referred to the converted runaway slave Onesimus as a 'dear brother'. He wanted Philemon to treat him as a brother too. Why? It was because everyone who trusts in Jesus then becomes part of the family of God. Isn't it sad when there are family quarrels? Isn't it wonderful when family members support one another in sickness, in trouble, in need and when treated badly by others?

Think about the lovely words of Psalm 133.

Chapter 7: A Friend in Persia
Bible references: 1 Timothy 1:2; 2 Timothy 1:5; 3:15. Who have had the greatest influence on you so far in your life? Who do you see as role models? Who have encouraged you?

Charles Simeon was a great influence on Henry Martyn and a wonderful bond was formed between them. But sometimes people who are no longer living can deeply influence us. The life and diary of David Brainerd deeply affected Henry Martyn. Christian biography and accounts of missionaries can affect us too.

The question can of course be turned round. What kind of influence do you have on family and friends? Is it one for good or ill?

Chapter 8: The Clapham Sect
Bible references: Psalm 146:7-8; Isaiah 58:6-10. Is it only prominent celebrities, political activists and other opinion formers who care for the hungry and the oppressed? Of course not. God cares, as Psalm 146 shows.

If God cares, then his people must care. This was true in Charles Simeon's day. They cared about slavery.

They cared about conditions in prisons. They cared about child labour – and much else.

But it is also true that there are numerous organisations established by Christians which help the oppressed, the hungry, the sick, the blind and the lonely. Do some research to find out about some of them. It would be a good idea to choose one which you can make a focus of prayer.

Chapter 9: Mission to the World
Bible references: Isaiah 6:8; Matthew 28:19-20.
How do you view Christian mission?

In Charles Simeon's day, travel was hazardous, medical treatment in case of illness was primitive, communication was limited, languages often had to be learned from scratch and communities could be aggressively hostile. Despite that, there was a sense of urgency to reach people with the good news of Jesus.

Do you think there is still a sense of urgency to tell people, whether in this country or abroad, about Jesus? Aren't there better opportunities through advances in travel, communications and the work of Bible translators?

To reach out, you need a love for Jesus and for people. People in mission organisations often work looking after children, teaching, nursing, working in an office, flying an aeroplane or in a host of other occupations which are different from the traditional image of a missionary hacking a path through the jungle.

You can reach out, too, to your school friends in many different ways.

If God calls you to do mission work, would you respond as Isaiah did?

Chapter 10: Charles Simeon and the Jews

Bible references: Romans 10:1.

Have you heard of anti-Semitism? It basically means hatred of the Jews. Its origins stretch back to the Bible. Just read the book of Esther. The worst modern example of it was the Holocaust during the Second World War in which it is reckoned that as many as six million Jews were put to death, many of them being gassed in the concentration camps such as Auschwitz. Eleven Israeli competitors were killed in a terrorist attack on them at the Munich games in 1972. Anti-Semitism is far from being in the past, however.

Why should Christians deplore anti-Semitism? Well, all of us, Jews and non-Jews, are God's creatures and to be respected as such. Anti-Semitism is a direct breach of the commandment to love our neighbour as ourselves. It is racism and bigotry. Jesus was a Jew, as were all the writers of the New Testament apart from Luke. The disciples were commanded to take the gospel first to the Jews and then to the Gentiles.

What can we do practically? We can pray for gospel work among Jewish people, such as the work done by the *International Mission to Jewish People*.

Chapter 11: Charles Simeon and the Church of England

Bible reference: Matthew 13:24-30.

No doubt you have heard the saying 'the grass is always greener on the other side of the fence'. It is true of churches. We can always think that this church or another will be much better, forgetting that churches are made up of sinners. Charles Simeon knew that the Church of England had many faults, but he appreciated its good points and was loyal to it.

Is loyalty considered much of a virtue or a desirable quality in this day and age? If someone dismissed loyalty as old-fashioned, what would you say in reply?

Chapter 12: His Wider Influence

Bible references: Matthew 5:13-16; Galatians 2:8-9; 3:28.

What experience have you of meeting and worshipping with Christians of other countries or backgrounds? Going to a different church can be a culture shock! But it can also show the breadth of the Kingdom of God and the bonds which link true believers together in the great Head of the Church.

The wonderful thing is that not only did Charles Simeon appreciate Christians from a different background, but that they appreciated him too. If he had adopted a stand-offish and aloof attitude, he would have robbed himself of the joy of leading the minister of Moulin to true spiritual understanding and effectiveness.

Salt spreads its preserving and savoury effect. Light spreads brightness. Let's be salt and light and look to see our witness spread.

Chapter 13: Preacher and Spiritual Guide

Bible reference: Hebrews 5:12-14; 1 Peter 2:2.

Do you study the Scriptures? It is easy to glance over a passage from the Bible as a daily reading without really giving it much thought or gaining much spiritual benefit. Charles Simeon had natural gifts and had gone through university, but still needed deep Bible study to sustain his own soul and his ministry.

How do we study the Scriptures? One way is to use a study Bible, which will help us understand difficult passages. Another way is to use study guides, which many publishers provide. Underlining important verses and learning them is another good strategy.

Chapter 14: Final Days

Bible reference: John 6:40; 14:1-3; 1 Corinthians 15:20-24.

Do you have a strong hope of heaven? Hope is a confident expectation, not wishful thinking. A strong hope makes us strong Christians and helps us cope with the stresses of the present.

To have a strong hope, we need to know what it is based on. Our hope is based on the resurrection of the Lord Jesus. Because he rose again from the dead we shall rise one day at the end of the world, if we have died before the Lord's return. It is also based on the Word of God. Jesus' promise is to raise up on the last day those who believe in him.

Treasure the sustaining, motivating hope of the gospel. It is a wonderful friend.

Note from the Author

Why write about Charles Simeon? The series is called Trail Blazers. In the unbelieving world of late eighteenth-century Cambridge, Charles Simeon certainly was a trailblazer. He came to a largely irreligious university (despite the outward forms of religion) but left it a place where, after his trailblazing, God and Jesus were once more honoured. So Charles Simeon 'fits the bill'.

Indeed, Charles Simeon was a thrilling example of how God can take one person and use that person wonderfully, despite his faults and failings. He was certainly an interesting character, but the reason he was so useful to God was surely his devotion to his Saviour, his love of the Scriptures, his commitment to prayer and his zeal

These are timeless qualities, but if there is one other quality shown by Charles Simeon so relevant today, it is his refusal to give way to discouragement. In a day of internet trolls when Bible-believing Christians are scorned, he is a wonderful role model, behaving with dignity when indignities were heaped on him. He neither caved in nor raged but calmly followed the example of the Saviour. So impressive!

Thomas Clarkson

The Giant With One Idea

Emily J. Maurits

- Biography for 9–14s
- British abolitionist
- Part of the successful Trail Blazers series

Thomas Clarkson was the son of a clergyman who lived in a time when it was legal to buy and sell slaves. He believed this was wrong, and campaigned to make sure this changed. He was instrumental in making sure that no human being could be bought or sold in the British Empire.

ISBN: 978-1-5271-0677-2

Robert Moffat

Africa's Brave Heart

Irene Howat

Robert Moffat could think on his feet, and use his hands. He was strong, practical and just the sort of guy you needed to back you up when you were in difficulty. Not only that, he had courage – loads of it, and a longing to bring the good news of Jesus Christ to the people of Africa.

As Robert faced the dangers of drought, wild animals and even the daggers and spears of the people he had come to help, he used his unique collection of gifts and attributes to spread the gospel.

Africa's brave heart blazed a trail into the unknown, starting a work in that continent that continues today.

ISBN: 978-1-84550-715-2

OTHER BOOKS IN THE
TRAIL BLAZERS SERIES

For a full list of Trail Blazers, please see our
website: www.christianfocus.com
All Trail Blazers are available as e-books